THE PLURALIST PARADIGM

THE PLURALIST PARADIGM:

Democracy and Religion in the 21st Century

Edited by

Sondra Myers and Patrice Brodeur

University of Scranton Press
Scranton and London

Library of Congress Cataloging-in-Publication Data

The pluralist paradigm: democracy and religion in the 21st century/
edited by Sondra Myers.
    p.   cm.
   Includes bibliographical references.
   ISBN 1-58966-151-6 (pbk.)
1. Democracy–Religious aspects.   2. Religious pluralism–Political
   aspects.
I. Myers, Sondra.
BL65.P7P58 2006
332'.1–dc22   2006050087

Distribution:

The University of Scranton Press
Chicago Distribution Center
11030 S. Langley
Chicago, IL 60628

PRINTED IN THE UNITED STATES OF AMERICA

Contents

Acknowledgements

I had the good fortune to have several extraordinary assistants in the course of my work on *The Pluralist Paradigm*. They gave me invaluable help in the research and organization of the book and have more than earned my gratitude for the intelligence, dedication, enthusiasm and good humor they brought to the project. Victoria Macchi, Lilly Deng, Anu Yadav, Ben Wastler, and Kim Liao worked diligently on preparing the manuscript, acquiring the permissions and giving generous support to "whatever it took" to get the book to the publisher. I am deeply in their debt.

In the last throes of the project, the superb staff of the Provost's office at the University of Scranton, Anne Marie Stamford, Mary Ann Maslar, Peggy Burke, and Brian Loughney rallied to the cause.

SM

Preface

The Pluralist Paradigm: Democracy and Religion in the 21ˢᵗ Century is long overdue on the one hand, and, on the other hand, richer, more comprehensive and even perhaps more optimistic because it has gestated for several years. The idea for the book came up in the fall of 2001, just after 9/11, when Patrice Brodeur and I met at a reception for Connecticut College alumni in Washington. Patrice was then an assistant professor of religious studies at the college with a specialty in Islam; I was an alumna and editor of the *Democracy is a Discussion* handbooks which were published by the college in 1996 and 1998. In the muddled moment of adjusting to a new level of uncertainty and anxiety about our personal and collective fates, we agreed to work together on a book that examined the relationship between democracy and religion, and, indeed, the classic struggle between state and church, or even putting democracy aside, Caesar and God.

The Pluralist Paradigm is the product of our joint effort involving a great deal of conversation, solitary reflection, and research. It continues the exploration into the growing influence and practice of democracy that we have witnessed in our time—in this instance, with regard to its juxtaposition to religion. What might have seemed an arcane issue some 30 years ago has become a subject that appears in the press on a daily basis in these times.

In the last fifteen years of the 20ᵗʰ century, we observed not only that democracy was on the move—with the end of the Cold War, the collapse of communism, and the disintegration or destabilization of a great number of totalitarian and authoritarian regimes—but that religion was on the move too. Fundamentalism was rearing its head, yes; but so were New-Age spiritualism, Pentecostalism, mainstream interfaith dialogue, and a dynamic cross-cultivation among religions of the east and west. In counterpoint to what sometimes resembled a tidal wave of fundamentalism, mainstream religions were breaking through the barriers of absolutism to accept not the religious beliefs of others, but the right of others to hold those beliefs. In the wake of the brutalities of the 20th century, it seemed that the time had come - that it was possible, practical and desirable - to coexist and even cooperate with people of different beliefs from one's own.

And we cannot omit from this profile of progress the significance of the revolution in information and communication technologies, which has permanently insinuated "the other" into our lives, and without which what is now a global exchange of ideas would be an enterprise on a dramatically reduced scale.

The delay, as it turns out, was fortuitous, if unintended, as, without it, we may have been driven to publish a book on fundamentalism, presuming that fundamentalism was the major religious feature of our day, and the primary cause of the events of 9/11 and the other acts of terror that were occurring with an almost rhythmic regularity around the world. That would have been too easy—much too oversimplified an explanation for the frightening and baffling events of our time. In retrospect one needs to ask whether it was religious zeal or political expediency, based on decades if not centuries of frustration and failure, that accounts for the eruptions of violence we have witnessed in recent times. There is no doubt that the geopolitical changes around the world left us with a vacuum, and a profound sense of vulnerability. The old world order was gone—and there was no new world order in sight. It is emerging, and given the dynamic of our time, it will continue to emerge and evolve at a rapid pace in the foreseeable future. We, as citizens, have the opportunity—even the obligation—to participate in shaping that new world order.

It is our hope that *The Pluralist Paradigm: Democracy and Religion in the 21st Century* will give us some guidance along the way. We see it as being on the continuum with the *Democracy is a Discussion* handbooks, which have been translated into a dozen languages and are used as a kind of primer on democracy in developing nations in every part of the world. Their use in the United States has been important as well, as we have, to our disadvantage, neglected to teach our nation's youth about the basic underpinnings of democracy, which give purpose and urgency to the civic actions and volunteerism that have been the hallmarks of our society.

Patrice and I realized that the move that religion has made to center stage during this period is an important if unexpected phenomenon and definitely worthy of analysis. Why has religion—in its myriad forms—become so prominent? Is it related to the political vacuum? The widening gap between the rich and poor? Does it reflect the rising tide of democracy? The somewhat chaotic in-between? The vapidity of materialism? The resistance to secularism? The loss of community in a globalized, McDonaldized world? What are the prospects for religion and democracy to coexist peacefully and collaborate creatively in our time?

These questions have driven us to uncover and focus on some of the many voices that can be heard speaking on the subject from a wide range of perspectives. One can find expressions of the idealism, the cynicism, and the pragmatism that play into the relationship between religion and democracy in the 21st century. The book is intended for believers and non-believers alike, as we are attempting to foster a respect for "the other," and the importance of making the effort to live peacefully and productively despite differences of religion or culture which are sure to crop up in our interdependent world.

Even as we in the US have become more polarized in our views and more insular in our ways, it makes sense for us as citizens to acknowledge our interdependence, and revive the public aspect of our lives. It is important to discuss the place that religion has in a democratic society, and the role democracy has in what Robert Bellah and his colleagues consider "a good society." It is not only necessary for the sustainability of a democratic society, but on a personal level, to stretch our hearts and minds on behalf of all the world's people. In *The Pluralist Paradigm,* we offer some insights into how we can develop a sound foundation for life in what can be a new democratic era by developing respectful, productive relationships between the democratic society and religion. Having a public life—and an active responsibility for the common good—gives greater breadth and depth to our existence. And while we see the public aspect of our lives as an obligation—it is an obligation that is in fact a rare privilege enjoyed by all too few.

Let us appreciate and celebrate the rights of all people to life and liberty, and assume the responsibility for ensuring that we extend those "inalienable" rights to the many. The task is vast, and eternal—and it is ours.

Sondra Myers
August, 2006

I
Introduction

Democracy and Religion:
An Overview of the Past, A Pluralist Vision for the Future

Patrice Brodeur

The task of this essay is fourfold: defining the meanings of the words democracy and religion, delimiting their respective contexts, analyzing their relationship in both theory and practice, and envisioning a pluralist paradigm for the future of their interrelatedness.

The relationship between democracy and religion is marked by conflicting visions that are often based on misunderstandings and false generalizations. It is one of the most urgent philosophical issues of our times, with often devastating impacts on local populations affected by various kinds of injustice. These conflicting visions fuel different forms of individual and collective violence: on the individual level, there is apathy, bullying, self-destructive behaviors (alcoholism, drugs, indiscriminate sex, etc), and ultimately suicide; on the collective organizational level, there is competition, double standards, inflated patriotism, religious self-righteousness, and wars. The combination of individual and collective forms of violence can lead to voluntary martyrdom, whether in the form of sporadic suicide bombings or systemic killings by state-sanctioned or interest-driven soldiers and freedom fighters, including thousands of child soldiers in the poorest areas of conflict.

The recent focus on terrorism worldwide, often diverting our attention from much older and more devastating civil wars, should be understood within the long history of human veneration of martyrdom. This veneration is embedded within a rhetoric of self-sacrifice for a "higher cause" common to a variety of worldviews, be they religious, secular, and/or democratic (the three not being mutually exclusive of one another). Indeed, twentieth-century wars have been fought by both dictatorial and democratic regimes, both religious and secular, to preserve and extend their own collective interests. In the name of democracy, religion, secularism, or a variety of other ideological "higher causes," the most pervasive currently being the idea of "the nation," countless human beings have been killed and wounded. Because of the competition between newer and more mature forms of non-religious ideologies (e.g. nationalism, socialism, communism, secularism) more human beings have been killed in the twentieth century than in the whole of prior human history.

This simple fact raises serious questions about the sources of violence. It forces all of us, whatever our worldview might be, to practice the art of self-examination and introspection. For those who claim that the problem is with religion, thereby using religion as a scapegoat, think twice. The reverse is equally true: for religious folks who think the problem is with a secular society, thereby using secularism as a scapegoat to explain all the ills of advanced democratic societies, think twice. And for those claiming allegiance to a worldview different from the normative Western one, who believe they can escape the Western-enlightenment polarization between religion and secularism by retrieving their own pre-colonial values and worldviews, think twice too: all worldviews today, to different degrees, are affected by the global competition over oil and water resources, among other material interests, and have been affected by the cancer of essentialist thinking underpinning the enlightenment paradigm of Western Europe in the late 18th and 19th centuries. This intellectual epidemic has spread through the seemingly innocuous modern sciences, and especially through its more popular and simplistic form of interpretation now called "scientism." The material power ascribed to the mostly useful discoveries of Western sciences has overshadowed many philosophical presuppositions about the nature of reality—presuppositions about objectivity, for example—that later infiltrated new modern developments in religious and secular discourse alike. On the religious side of this equation, essentialism is completely embedded in what is popularly known as fundamentalism. On the secular side, essentialism is present in the guise of patriotic nationalism, scientism, and secular fundamentalism.

From the outset, I draw the reader's attention to these serious misrepresentations in understanding democracy and religion in order to avoid two extremes: demonization or adulation of any one "higher cause," be it religion, secularism, or democracy, the three main elements of this article.

Defining Democracy and Religion

As Robert Dahl pointed out in his famous introductory book *On Democracy*, "When we discuss democracy perhaps nothing gives rise to more confusion that the simple fact that democracy refers to both an ideal and an actuality. We often fail to make the distinction clear." (Dahl, 26) The same can be said of religion. In addition, both concepts carry a variety of definitions on a theoretical level and a variety of measuring scales on a practical level.

Let us begin with democracy. When we define democracy today, we certainly do not refer to the theoretical assumptions that guided the practices of men who shared an Athenian citizenship over two thousand years ago and met in an assembly to pitch their names into a lottery system out of which their political and military leadership would emerge. Nor do we mean the twelfth-century thoughts and practices encountered in the first three cantons of what is now called Switzerland. Ideally today, democracy includes five criteria: effective participation, equality in voting, gaining enlightened understanding, exercising final control over the agenda, and inclusion of adults within a finite set of national boundaries and citizenship. (Dahl, 38) These criteria are linked to values such as "avoiding tyranny, essential rights, general freedom, self-determination, moral autonomy, human development, protecting essential personal interests, political equality, . . . peace-seeking, prosperity." (Dahl, 45)

These ideals do not exist in pure form anywhere today, even in advanced democracies. If we are going to compare different forms of democracy, the comparison of its ideal forms must be conducted separately from comparisons of current practices. This overview essay focuses on neither of these comparisons; rather it raises a variety of issues to be considered when making comparisons on these two different levels.

Another common problem is that too often the above modern idealistic understanding of democracy is projected backward in time in search of its historical origins. The search for origins is linked to an attempt to find the "essential" elements that constitute the core or essence of democracy. These efforts often turn out to be futile, at least in their initial intent. The danger in such a search for origins lies in its results: a misconception that democracy developed only in the West. This distortion then fuels the notion that only the West can today "export" democracy because it never existed anywhere else. Logically, we are faced with a tautology: by defining democracy only

5

according to what emerged in the West and looking for its origins only in a narrow geographical set of historical possibilities, it stands to reason that the search for origins only results in what was set out to be proven in the first place. Scientists across the disciplines are now aware that their theoretical and methodological assumptions predetermine the outcomes of their research. The long term methodological solution is to enlarge the set of theoretical references within any given scientific dialogue to include experts and practitioners from as broad a range of identities and personal histories as possible.

I suggest dividing democracy into three categories: proto-democracy, modern democracy, and "glocal" democracy. (For a definition of "glocal", see Brodeur, 188). The first includes all forms of collective decision-making based on popular participation. Defined this way, the historical search for early forms of democracy is not limited to a linguistic genealogy that privileges the Eurocentric search for origins. Instead, proto-democracies are found in political systems across space and time that demonstrate similar characteristics and values to those that existed in the proto-democracies of fifth century BCE Athens and twelfth century CE proto-Switzerland, for example. Indeed, this kind of proto-democracy did not disappear in many parts of the world less affected by modern development. For example, it is being rediscovered in many villages throughout Mali by Professor Ousmane Sy as part of his research on what constitutes good governance in sub-Saharan Africa.

The second, modern democracy, is what we mean by democracy today, when we assume that democracy must take place within the structures of a nation-state, with all the criteria and values mentioned above. The third, glocal democracy, refers to what I envision to be the unfolding democratization process that affects all spheres of life in multiple directions today. These directions include the dissemination of various forms of democracy through different sectors of society locally, and at the same time, transcend the present borders of nation-states to affect international organizations and transnational movements.

The same threefold distinction of the word religion can be used in order to organize the countless definitions of religion that emerged in the twentieth century. Proto-religion includes all pre-modern forms of collective human behavior that combine myths and rituals to make sense of reality. Modern religion refers to all proto-religion forms that have survived into or have grown up in the twentieth century, adapting themselves to the powerful forces of modernization including individualism, essentialism, democratization, materialism/consumerism, objectification, and tourism. "Glocal" religion refers to newly emerging forms of religiosity and spirituality that transcend the boundaries of religious identities. These new developments occur in various sectors of society locally as much as globally, in both distinct and similar fashions, due to technologically advanced methods of communication that transcend the geographical limitations in space, and even in time.

Contextualizing Democracy and Religion

The task before us in the twenty-first century is no longer to find either the "right" definition on a theoretical level among existing ones or by proposing a better one as I have done heuristically above, or the "right" set of measuring tools by which to judge the phenomena of democracy and religion in actuality. Rather, the current task is threefold.

First, we need to uncover the history of how each word came to develop, that is, describe the genealogy of its meanings over time, going back two and a half millennia to the early Greek experiment in Athens. In other words, concepts, like people, have genealogies that need to be discovered in order to understand them better.

Second, we need to demonstrate the interrelationship between particular definitions and sets of measuring tools for both democracy and religion, as well as their close interdependence in their initial Western historical context. Their respective yet closely related genealogies belong to sister languages within the broader Indo-European family of languages: the word "democracy" developed out of the Greek *demokratia* and "religion" out of the Latin *religio*. (For a full history of the Latin origins and transformations in meanings of the word *religio*, see WC Smith). Similar forms and pronunciations now exist with the same etymology in modern Greek and Latin-based languages (Italian, Spanish, Portuguese, French, and Romanian), with easily traceable cognates in all neighboring Indo-European languages, such as English, German, and Dutch, as well as Scandinavian and Slavic languages. Both words were eventually adopted into the unique language family loosely connecting Hungarian and Finnish. In short, both the words have migrated into all European languages, irrespective of the language families.

Third, we need to analyze how the genealogies of democracy and religion, which are rooted in a particular Western history and a set of Western-based languages, have imposed or insinuated themselves around the world during the colonial and post-colonial periods up to our day. This last task raises a multitude of comparative interpretive challenges of an inter-civilizational nature. Democracy and religion are concepts and experiences that were appropriated and/or imposed variously in different parts of the world during the nineteenth and twentieth centuries by a few Western countries (UK, France, Netherlands, Portugal, Spain, Russia/USSR, USA, and to a lesser degree Italy and Germany). This historical process continues to unfold as more and more people learn English as the now normative language of what is often referred to as "the international community."

A look into how the two concepts of democracy and religion have been translated into non-Western languages is often a window into a variety of very different concepts that only approximate the meanings that emerged in Western history. These various concepts in a multitude of non-Western languages also have their own complex genealogies, linked to particular histories that do not reproduce Western history. Yet, they often demonstrate alternative forms of government with equally important values for collective political decision-making. For example, there is the southern African concept of "ubuntu":

> . . . a philosophy of life, which in its most fundamental sense represents personhood, humanity, humaneness and morality; a metaphor that describes group solidarity where such group solidarity is central to the survival of communities with a scarcity of resources. It is not enough to refer to the meaning and profound concept of ubuntuism merely as a social ideology. Ubuntu is the very quality that guarantees not only a separation between men, women and the beast, but the very fluctuating gradations that determine the relative quality of that essence. It is for that reason that we prefer to call it the potential of being human. (Mokgoro)

Ubuntu emerged as an alternative conceptual language during the struggle against apartheid in South Africa. It is now at the heart of the post-apartheid South African approach to democracy and it acts as a powerful philosophical influence in the democratic processes sweeping across sub-Saharan Africa today.

Another example is the Arabic word "shûrâ," meaning "consultation" or "deliberation." It is frequently used in majority Muslim countries, especially in the Arab world, in the expression "majlis al-shûrâ" to refer to "parliament." The concept of "shûrâ" is pre-Islamic, going back to a very old Arab tribal practice of communal decision-making by a small group of elders who represented the most important clans within a tribe. This practice was islamized by the Prophet Muhammad during his leadership of the first Islamic community between 622 and

632, when he died. It was continued during the lives of four subsequent leaders until 661, not without other forms emerging to challenge it at a time of great transformation in this nascent and rapidly expanding community. While the concept was integrated into aspects of Islamic law (shari'ah), its practice in subsequent centuries continued relatively unchanged in tribal areas, with major transformations in more urban areas, while it disappeared in others. The concept of "shûrâ" was retrieved in the second half of the twentieth century by many Muslims who wanted to respond to the Western criticism that Islam is undemocratic. Some apologists superficially claimed that the early Islamic community was democratic because it practiced "shûrâ" or consultation. Such a claim is like saying that six-century Athenians were democratic, not understanding that the definition and practice of democracy then did not correspond to how it is understood and practiced today, although general parallels do exist. Other contemporary Muslims are striving to reinterpret *shûrâ* in light of democratic norms having emerged first in the West but that are now part of much of the world's growing expectations of what good governance is all about. Instead of simply adopting terminology that is directly translated from Western languages ("dimûqrâtîyah" for "democracy", for example), this old concept of *shûrâ* was retrieved and reinterpret to make sense of contemporary needs and expectations within an interdependent world of nation-states. These two examples reflect two modern responses to processes of indigenization as related to the concept of democracy. Parallel processes exist with the ways in which the word "religion" was indigenized into a variety of non-European languages under the impact of Western colonialism.

Today, we must take the time to analyze those translations and find those conceptual cognates in languages other than English and closely related European languages in order to insure that the democratic wind blowing across the world today is not imposing a Western kind of democracy. The construction of a true international community requires respect for the very different perspectives through which Western notions of democracy and religion are seen when coming into contact with other more or less similar concepts across various other civilizational identities.

A parallel example from the field of sustainable development is useful: scholars and practitioners alike make a clear distinction between modernization and Westernization. When the two overlap, local resistance emerges. For example, if modernization requires people

9

to produce only Western-looking cars, clothes, and architectural styles because the technology comes initially from the West, the processes of modernization rapidly destabilize local production means and the new material culture is perceived as foreign and is likely to be rejected, especially by those who cannot afford it. When the two are distinguished, there is much less resistance. For example, when the material processes of modernization (i.e. technology) can be adopted within the local cultural norms and values of a given society, local resistance is minimized. It is important to note, however, that this resistance is never completely absent because any form of technology exported beyond its initial social context carries with it, at least minimally, cultural assumptions that get integrated into the host environment. History is full of such examples, from the invention of paper and fireworks in China to the cultivation of corn and potatoes in the Americas, the production of which had already spread to many areas of the world long before the twentieth century.

When translating this example back into the area of religion and democracy, we find that more and more scholars and practitioners clearly distinguish between the broad concept of democracy, often popularly simplified to "one person, one vote", and Western democracy, often predominantly idealized in the current yet very different American, French, and British models. If current worldwide processes of democratization, consciously or not, promote only Western models of democracy, thereby making democracy and Westernization synonymous, local resistance emerges. For example, certain forms of extremist Islamic religious discourses, among others, associate democracy simplistically with neo-liberal and Christian missionary aims and falsely with Jewish conspiracy theories to control the world. When democracy is promoted by way of a principle of contextualization, that is, respecting the local cultural/religious context within which the values of individual participation in the political decision-making process of a country's governance can be interpreted and implemented, then there is much less resistance. In fact, it may even be done beyond existing nation-states, as with some pan-Islamic, pan-Turkic, and pan-European ideologies.

In short, as a family of Western models developed over the last three hundred years in the West, what I call the "Western family of democracies", it stands to reason that there also emerged a variety of civilizational families of democracies within other geographical areas around the world: For example, we can think of a Confucian family of democracies in East and Southeast Asia, an Islamic family of democracies across majority Muslim countries from Morocco to Indonesia, an Indian family of democracies in South Asia, an African family of democracies in sub-Saharan Africa, and some Caribbean islands, a Latin American family of democracies, and an Indigenous family of democracies scattered worldwide. This list is by no means exhaustive, but it will serve as a framework to organize the next section of this article.

Three additional factors complicate the picture described so far. First, the broad geographical references given to the family names above have limited usefulness since some of these families spread across very different geographical areas (for example, Australia and New Zealand being part of Western democracies). Second, a growing number of immigrants and seasonal workers in numerous countries are creating transnational realities that affect the geographical homogeneity of older and emerging democracies. Finally, many older democracies need to contend with their historical relationship to indigenous communities and must adopt new forms of democracy that integrate traditional indigenous worldviews and practices. The best example of the latter is New Zealand/Aotearoa. Thus, the geographical referent to most of these family names must be understood in light of these important limitations.

A second factor in determining how we can understand democracy and religion is the power dynamic within which these democratic and religious developments are emerging since the end of the Cold War in 1990. The wind of democratization that has followed cannot be isolated from the already-growing awareness in the West of a worldwide phenomenon referred to in French as "le retour du religieux" (the return of the religious). In many areas of the world, though not all, these two late twentieth century developments are completely intertwined and explain why this book is so important.

On the one hand, Western democracies and large oil-producing nations are the two most powerful groups of nation-states in the world at present, with the principal exceptions of China and Japan. On the other hand, Christianity and Islam are the two most numerous religious communities in terms of demography and the two most powerful discursive religious systems in the world. When these powerful nations contain either a Christian or a Muslim dimension, in one form or another, the mix can easily lead to a double standard and/or a paternalism in the way they project their own normative understanding of what democracy or religion ought to be when they are engaged in the promotion of democracy or religion in what are called "emerging democracies". Even the scholarly nomenclature is not without its legacy of paternalism and Western-centrism. For lack of better words, this international and interreligious power dynamic infiltrates all aspect of human life today. Any effort to understand democracy and religion and the relationship between the two requires a framework which must take these forces into account.

Yet a third factor must be added. As great as the above-mentioned nation-states and religious forces are, a few multinationals can be equally if not more powerful than the largest national economies of the USA, Japan and Germany, for example. The latest era of post-modernism is one in which, on a global level, several pre-modern characteristics (eg. feudalism, slavery, centralized and despotic rulers, concentration of wealth) co-exist side by side with modern ones (e.g. nation-state, rule of law, democracy, financial regulation). It is clear that if we were to analyze democracy and religion only within their initial modern framework of the nation-state, the results would not be adequate to explain the wide variety of discrepancies that are emerging around the world in practice and the very polemical debates they represent in theory. The only possible way to analyze the present state of affairs in terms of democracy and religion is to frame it on a planetary level and examine the interdependent forces that promote, transform, resist, or curtail their various lively forms today.

Analyzing Democracy and Religion in Theory and Practice

Analyzing democracy and religion in theory and practice is like going through an archaeological dig; the only difference is that instead of digging through layers of soil to discover specific objects whose style and form help us determine their date and provenance, we dig through layers of meanings attached to words that can be found only in surviving texts written and transcribed in different historical periods. This textual analysis uncovers how these two English words came to appear from a long genealogy of two and a half millennia going back to early forms of the Greek and Latin languages. While this particular archaeological dig into European history is unavoidable for this overview essay, other digs will be necessary elsewhere to uncover the rich heritage of proto-democracy that has existed in vastly different cultures and regions of the world up to the present, as mentioned earlier. As is the case for most histories of democracy available today in Western languages, failing to do this comparative historical "archaeology" limits the readers to reproduce a

Western superiority bias. By not seeking to compare how similar (or not) co-extensive forms of human government existed across the world at any given point in time, contemporary researchers may end up reading history through their own eyes, only reinforcing their present sense of superiority. Yet, the worldwide diversity of contemporary interpretations of the concept of democracy in both theory and practice today can not be done outside the impact of the specific Western history of the changing meanings of the word "democracy" over time.

The word "democracy" first appeared in Greece from the combination of "demos" (people) and "kratos" (to rule). In 507 BCE, the city-state of Athens adopted a democratic system that lasted for about two centuries until it fell under the control of the Macedonian, Alexander the Great, in 321 BCE. Other city-states in Greece developed similar models, but much less is known about them. Athens has passed down in Western history as the principal model for democracy because it resulted in a creative culture out of which emerged key philosophical figures (Plato, Aristotle, Socrates, etc.) and later writings that shaped the development of Mediterranean and, more broadly speaking, Western history down to our times. The people that were allowed to participate in this kind of popular government were all the men who had Athenian citizenship; women were excluded. It was indeed a popular democracy, what we call today a participatory democracy, at least for half the population. Citizens met in a popular assembly and many of the highest positions, including those in the army, were elected by lottery. While the lottery system did not survive the Athenian experiment, many other characteristics of this popular system of government did.

At about the same time in Rome, the republic system emerged, from "res" (thing or affair) and "publicus" (public). Only male aristocrats could initially participate in this republic; much later, and after much struggle, the common men gained access. The rights of Roman citizenship were eventually extended to worthy conquered peoples, but the decision-making assembly remained based in Rome, making it difficult for new citizens, often living far away, to participate. The size of the assembly and its participation mechanism were never adapted to the republic's changing needs; the Romans "never developed a workable system of *representative* government based on *democratically elected* representatives." (Dahl, 14) The Roman republic lasted longer than the Athenian one. Unlike its older Athenian sister that died from external takeover by the Macedonians, the Roman experiment, with its republican form of proto-democracy, collapsed from internal decay from 130 BCE onward due to "civil unrest, war, militarization, corruption, and a decline in the sturdy civic spirit that had previously existed among its citizens." (Dahl, 14)

These causes and their effects are a striking reminder of what has proven to be the case in more recent history, such as that which led to World War I and, in some respect, to World War II, when some of the principal belligerent nation-states included democracies. With the Cold War, the dangers presented by the emphasis on a strong external enemy created a double standard within Western bloc democracies as they practiced democracy within their own nation-states while often supporting or tolerating undemocratic regimes outside in order to protect interests at the national level and also to expand the geopolitical sphere of influence. With the end of the Cold War, the capitalist and more democratic Western alliance won the day. Yet, the momentum of the old logic of "needing a common enemy" did not disappear overnight. It has resurfaced in the form of a new enemy, Islam, attenuated more recently to "Islamism," a modern ideological form of Islamic political discourse, not unlike earlier mid-twentieth century Western national political discourses of a fascist kind.

The reaction of the most powerful current democracy, the USA, to the terrorist attacks of September 11, 2001, especially with the Patriot Act, has raised questions about the changing interpretations of where the limits of democracy lie depending on the political climate at any particular period in a country's history. The culture of fear, both initially real and later sustained, has been an important factor in these interpretations. A similar phenomenon has started to unfold recently in England and in other countries directly affected by recent terrorist attacks. One important exception among Western democratic nations is Spain, which is probably due to its own long history of having to deal with terrorist attacks from Basque separatists.

In addition to all the historical factors and especially the recent political contexts that vary from one country to another, these examples raise the important question of what constitutes an appropriate emotional climate for any country that either is, has started, or hopes to become democratic. Trying to make sense of this question requires an interdisciplinary approach that combines social psychology with at least three other fields of study: history, political science, and religious studies.

Religious studies scholars have demonstrated that there is a direct link between the rise of certain forms of extreme religiosity and the real or perceived insecurity among large segments of a population at different times and places in human history. For example, the proximity of millennial expectations, especially in Western Christianity around the year 1000 and, to a lesser degree among Shi'ite Muslims around the year 1000 of the Islamic hijra calendar (ca. 1600 CE), gave rise to such forms of eschatological religiosity whereby fears of future calamities enable particular forms of political authority to take hold of large segments of the population. Scholars of contemporary religious phenomena witnessed these trends a few years ago with the coming of the year 2000 CE and the Y2K threat of technological mayhem. (Landes). This gave rise to a global insecurity that had barely had time to subside when it was replaced by the widespread reactions of fear, especially in the West, following the terrorist attacks of September 11, 2001. The subsequent global war on terrorism ignited the embers of the Y2K threat in both the educated elites of the international community and in popular consciousness in many areas around the world, with important local variations. The subsequent culture of fear that this war on terrorism has fuelled helps sustain the grassroots support for greater militarization in many democratic nations and emerging democracies in the world. Indeed, there has been a political shift to the right across most democratic countries in recent years, especially in Western Europe. The increased military budgets that often follow these shifts affect the social welfare systems negatively, leading to increased xenophobia and the long term degradation of the social fabric that is required in order to sustain a civic culture without which a citizen-based participatory democracy cannot survive. In addition, natural calamities such as the recent hurricanes and earthquakes that take up so much of the international media's coverage (though not without gross discrepancies in regional coverage) also contribute to forms of religiosity that help people make sense of an otherwise senseless world. Finally, the catastrophic scenario promoted by extreme environmentalists also fuels the sense of global insecurity and becomes a double edge sword easily manipulated by extreme religious and political voices alike.

We are facing a global co-dependency between, on the one hand, religious discourses that promote, openly or covertly, exclusive eschatological visions of an end of time that is near and where only the "righteous ones" can be saved and, on the other hand, political discourses that promote a self-righteous, paternalistic, and exclusivist nationalist vision that intends to protect its citizens from outside threats. The result can be seen in a negative spiral fuelled by increased competition in all spheres of life: from saving souls (competing missionary movements) to saving the planet, passing through increased commodification of human beings and other forms of life in a hyper-competitive global economy.

Envisioning a Pluralist Paradigm for the Future of Democracy and Religion

Faced with this dire situation, we need to envision the future of democracy and religion imaginatively. In this vain, I envision a pluralist paradigm for the conceptual relationship between democracy and religion that takes the plurality of both individual and collective identities and worldviews as well as the values of justice and equity seriously, within their respective genealogies and histories that remain always embedded in power dynamics reflected in changing language use and meanings. Moving towards such a pluralist paradigm requires us to transcend the binary reductions that often frame present interpretations of these two concepts, as if they were mutually exclusive. It is in part the result of both the crisis of the holy, that is, the failure of large segments of religious communities to prioritize sustainable human values and behaviors above their own collective religious identity interests, and the crisis of the nation-state, that is, the failure of large segments of national communities to prioritize sustainable human values and behaviors above their own collective national identity interests. The present essay has hopefully demonstrated the dangers of this reductive perception of the complex reality of the interrelationship between democracy and religion over several centuries. Instead, I propose a pluralist paradigm that includes at least six elements.

First, a pluralist paradigm distinguishes between, on the one hand, the plurality (or diversity) of identities and worldviews (which includes religious and/or spiritual as well as ideological and/or philosophical perspectives) which has always existed in human history and, on the other, the ideology-philosophy of pluralism, which is the contemporary challenge to learn how to live sustainably with this plurality of identities and worldviews. As long as reductive exclusivist national and religious interests dominate political agendas within both national discourses (whether secular, religious, or a combination of both) and religious ones (whether theologies or philosophies) because the plurality of identities and worldviews is perceived as a threat in the absence of clearly articulated alternative inclusive political and religious agendas, the logic of fear that has infiltrated large segments of overlapping national and religious communities will continue to fuel the rationale for increased militarism and protectionist national policies, further undermining democratic practices. This situation only exacerbates the double standard of promoting democracy within the national boundaries of one's own democratic nation-state but not necessarily abroad, as mentioned earlier. It also makes changes towards sustainable political decision-making in all spheres of life very difficult. The partial national exceptions to this situation are New Zealand, Costa Rica, and Sweden, all three of which have or are, in different ways, in the process of demilitarizing and promoting sustainable societies.

Second, a pluralist paradigm recognizes that both democracy and religion are fluid in meaning and diverse in reality and that these changes in meanings and on-the-ground realities occur out of changing perceptions of what our collective human needs are within today's international power dynamics. To the two examples of *ubuntu* and *shûrâ* briefly studied earlier in this essay, further analysis of other parallel terms from Chinese, Indian, etc., and various indigenous worldviews await to be added in order to enrich my all-too-superficial first attempt to develop a more inclusive framework to interpret democracy and religion.

Third, a pluralist paradigm acknowledges that the present tensions between the plurality of interpretations of the concepts of democracy and religion have emerged out of a particular Western history that have pitted different forms of secularism and, initially, European Christianity against one another and that this tension has now been globalized through colonialism and post-colonialism, forcing other civilizational histories to position themselves vis-à-vis this Western historical tension between democratic and religious values consciously or unconsciously imposed within the international community.

Fourth, a pluralist paradigm requires an ethical commitment to integrate rather than segregate the multiple identities and worldviews that shape the diverse responses worldwide to the concepts of democracy and religion. This integration allows for local interpretations rooted in local genealogies to carry the weight of interpretations and applications, emphasizing inter-dependence and complementarity in power dynamics rather than either imposition and independence from, or co-dependence with, the small number of current powerful national and multi-national players. For interdependence to be more effective in human relations today, democratic practices must be integrated into all forms of human interaction, from the family and local community levels to those of the school, the neighbourhood, the town or city, the region, province, state, national, or transnational institutions. Indeed, every human being and identity group must realize that his or her own survival and quality of life depends on that of others, in a glocal web of inter-dependence. This in-depth transformation, already started in small pockets of innovative change scattered around the world, is the best option for a truly sustainable security for all; it helps reduce the present trend that would have our collective survival be based on competitive and exclusivist patterns of behavior (i.e. "survival of the fittest" for the holders of a neo-liberal worldview and "survival of the rightly guided and believing" for those of an exclusivist religious worldviews) rather than cooperative ones.

Fifth, a pluralist paradigm encourages both national and religious institutions, among others, to change systemically so as to facilitate greater individual participation in decision-making on the basis that notions of rights and responsibilities as citizens need to be expanded to include not only national discourses and practices but also religious, economic, and other sectors of human activity. Indeed, there is an urgent need to educate towards global citizenship in all national educational systems worldwide, so that human beings can add to their existing set of multiple identities the awareness of an additional layer, that of our common humanity. The latest developments in the science of education point to the benefits of developing democratic practices in the classroom of schools, university, and other educational institutions, whether formal or informal, from the earliest age onwards. Similarly, by enhancing the quality of individual participation within religious institutions, both religious communities in particular and societies in general will benefit.

For this to happen, three forms of dialogue are necessary: intra-religious, inter-religious, and inter-worldview (between religious and other forms of worldviews, often mistakenly reduced to "secular"). These different forms of dialogue reduce the exclusivist worldviews that are the root causes of the cycle of violence, which begins with the arrogance of holding on to one's perspective as Truth, to stereotyping the Other, then vilifying, demonizing, dehumanizing, and ultimately killing the Other in the name of various transcending concepts, be they called god, nirvana, brahman, nation, progress, freedom of the market, science, race, tribe, ethnicity, etc. The increase of dialogical practices in education in particular and in deliberative practices in all spheres of life in general can only improve democratic practices in both national educational systems as well as in religious communities. This dialogical learning produces a new generation of human beings who have integrated the competencies required to insure that they not be manipulated by various forms of exclusivist ideologies, theologies, or philosophies. These human beings can reflect rationally and compassionately when weighing the information necessary to make their choices in all spheres of life. Harnessing over time this incredible potential wealth of individual decision-making power in the realms of material, intellectual, emotional, and spiritual consumption will promote improved democratic practices and ethical values in all spheres of life, leading to a more just and thereby peaceful world.

Finally, a pluralist paradigm acknowledges that our human sustainability on earth must go through a paradigm shift from the current normative competitive neo-liberal global power dynamics to a future cooperative glocal dynamics based on truly share human values and sustainable practices. This paradigm shift requires a thorough self-examination of our personal and collective behavior, belief, and thinking patterns on the basis of values shared by all cultures and religions: humility, justice, compassion, honesty, cooperation, and the search for Truth through dialogue. In brief, to improve democratic practices worldwide, it is necessary to articulate more carefully the interdependence between secular and religious understandings of democracy. In simple terms, it is false to think that "religion is part of the problem"; instead, it is better to think that "religion is part of the solution", in the sense that various religious political worldviews can adapt over time to democratic values, in a complementary rather than competitive way.

In such an imagined pluralist future, the present tensions between too often competing interpretations of the concepts of democracy and religion are transcended to make room for inclusive interpretations rooted in the integration of all human genealogies and histories, trying to avoid linguistic, philosophical, ideological, or religious forms of imperialism and paternalism. This visionary task has begun as a global multi-lingual, inter-civilizational, and democratic conversation unfolds, reflected in the brief, but all too incomplete, range of accompanying articles and excerpts from diverse thinkers on democracy and religion. The philosophical and ethical challenge of developing a pluralist paradigm for the future of democracy as it relates to religion requires greater inter-worldview dialogue between individuals and communities that have acquired solid knowledge of more than their own histories and worldviews. This dialogue can help bridge the present gaps of misunderstandings that fuel the violence and terrorism that result from different forms of exclusion and injustice. The role of education in this process of acquiring the dialogue skills necessary to acquire this bridging knowledge is crucial. The various articles and excerpts that follow in this book, when read and discussed in local groups, will activate collective envisioning of what is best conceptualized globally on the basis of what is most pragmatically needed and applied locally. It is my hope that the cumulative effect of these local dialogues worldwide will stimulate a glocal synergy from which will emerge over the next decades new forms of pluralist democracies inter-dependent of one another worldwide and sustainable for the whole human race.

Bibliography:

Brodeur, Patrice. "From Postmodernism to 'Glocalism': Towards a Theoretical Understanding of Contemporary Arab Muslim Constructions of Religious Others," in *Globalization and the Muslin World*, ed. by Birgit Schaebler and Leif Stenberg. Syracuse: Syracuse University Press, 2004, 188-205.

Dahl, Robert A. *On Democracy*. New Haven: Yale University Press, 1998.

Landes, Richard. "Owls and Roosters: Y2K and Millennium's End." Boston, Center for Millennial Studies at Boston University, 1998.

Mokgoro, JY. "Ubuntu and the Law in South Africa," from: http://www.puk.ac.za/lawper/1998-1/mokgoro-2.html

O'Donnell, Guillermo and J.V. Cullel and O.M. Iazzetta, eds. *The Quality of Democracy: Theory and Applications*. South Bend, IN: University of Notre Dame Press, 2004.

Smith, WC. *The Meaning and End of Religion*. New York: Macmillan, 1963.

Discussion Questions for the Introduction

1. What is essentialism? What, according to Patrice Brodeur, are the religious, secular, and democratic manifestations of it? What are the disadvantages or dangers of embracing an essentialist world-view?

2. Discuss the characteristics of Brodeur's three categories of democracy: proto-democracy, modern democracy, and glocal democracy. What are the distinctions of glocal democracy that make it a possible model for the future?

3. Discuss the characteristics of the three distinct categories of religion: proto-religion, modern religion and glocal religion. Why does the glocal form of religion seem to fit the future?

4. How does the African concept of *obuntu* stand apart from the western ideas of democracy and religion? Similarly, how does the Arabic word, *"shûrâ"* elude the western definitions of democracy and religion?

5. When are western notions of democracy and religion accepted in non-westernized societies?

6. Why is it essential to acknowledge cultural differences even when looking for common bonds among people?

7. What impact did the "culture of fear," following the terrorist attacks of 9/11/01, have on democracy and civic culture, and on religion in the United States, and to a lesser degree, in the West?

8. Were the 9/11 attacks and the increased incidence of terrorism in the first years of the 21st century a result of a revival of religious fundamentalism, of frustration and anger, or of a clash of civilizations?

9. Given the escalation of violence in our time, and its complex underlying causes, where can we turn for hope?

10. What is the role of education in strengthening democracy, tolerance, and the culture of interdependence? The role of religious institutions?

11. Using the institutions that are basic to our societies, and employing our human gifts of intellect, imagination and moral and civic sensibilities, can we become a more sane and humane world in the 21st century?

12. According to Brodeur, what are the six most important points of his pluralist paradigm through which we may re-envision the future relationship between democracy and religion?

II - A

Democracy and Religion:
In Creative Tension, Perennial
Conflict, or Constructive Interaction?

The selections in this section acknowledge the capacity of religion to be harmful as well as helpful to individuals and society. They stand as a set of useful warnings about the negative capacities of religion without proposing a doctrinaire rejection of religion as a powerful force in the history of the world. This section aims to lay open the enormous range of influences that religion can have on societies and that societies can have on religion. Ultimately it points readers in the direction of the pluralist paradigm. It demonstrates the diversity of religious beliefs and systems that exist in the world, and the ecological benefits of diversity, be it physical, as in nature, spiritual, as in religious and non-religious spiritual enterprises, and political, as in the myriad ways that human beings organize their societies.

Desecularization of the World

Peter Berger

The questions posed for discussion in this volume concern the relation of the religious resurgence to a number of issues not linked to religion.

- First, *international politics*. Here one comes up head-on against the thesis, eloquently proposed not long ago by Samuel Huntington, that, with the end of the Cold War, international affairs will be affected by a "clash of civilizations" rather than by ideological conflicts. There is something to be said for this thesis. The great ideological conflict that animated the Cold War is certainly dormant for the moment, but I, for one, would not bet on its final demise. Nor can we be sure that new ideological conflicts may not arise in the future. To the extent that nationalism is an ideology (more accurately, each nationalism has its *own* ideology), ideology is alive and well in a long list of countries.

    It is also plausible that, in the absence of the overarching confrontation between Soviet Communism and the America-led West, cultural animosities suppressed during the Cold War period are surfacing. Some of these animosities have themselves taken on an ideological form, as in the assertion of a distinctive Asian identity by a number of governments and intellectual groups in East and Southeast Asia. This ideology has become especially visible in debates over the allegedly ethnocentric/Eurocentric character of human rights as propagated by the United States and other Western governments and governmental organizations. But it would probably be an exaggeration to see these debates as signaling a clash of civilizations. The situation closest to a religiously defined clash of civilizations would come about if the world-view of the most radical branches of the Islamic resurgence came to be established within a wider spectrum of countries and became the basis of the foreign policies of these countries. As yet this has not happened.

To assess the role of religion in international politics, it would be useful to distinguish between political movements that are genuinely inspired by religion and those that use religion as a convenient legitimation for political agendas based on quite non-religious interests. Such a distinction is difficult but not impossible. Thus there is no reason to doubt that the suicide bombers of the Islamic Haws movement truly believe in the religious motives they avow. By contrast, there is good reason to doubt that the three parties involved in the Bosnian conflict, commonly represented as a clash between religions, are really inspired by religious ideas. I think it was P. J. O'Rourke who observed that these three parties are of the same race, speak the same language, and are distinguished only by their religion, which none of them believe. The same skepticism about the religious nature of an allegedly religious conflict is expressed in the following joke from Northern Ireland: As a man walks down a dark street in Belfast, a gunman jumps out of a doorway, holds a gun to his head, and asks, "Are you Protestant or Catholic?" The man stutters, "Well, actually, I'm an atheist." "Ah yes," says the gunman, "but are you a Protestant or a Catholic atheist?"

• Second, *war and peace*. It would be nice to be able to say that religion is everywhere a force for peace. Unfortunately, it is not. Very probably religion in the modern world more often fosters war, both between and within nations. Religious institutions and movements are fanning wars and civil wars on the Indian subcontinent, in the Balkans, in the Middle East, and in Africa, to mention only the most obvious cases. Occasionally, indeed, religious institutions try to resist warlike policies or to mediate between conflicting parties. The Vatican mediated successfully in some international disputes in Latin America. There have been religiously inspired peace movements in several countries (including the United States, during the Vietnam War). Both Protestant and Catholic clergy have tried to mediate the conflict in Northern Ireland, though with notable lack of success.

But it is probably a mistake to look here simply at the actions of formal religious institutions or groups. There may be a diffusion of religious values in a society that could have peace-prone consequences even in the absence of formal actions by church bodies. For example, some analysts have argued that the wide diffusion of

Christian values played a mediating role in the process that ended the apartheid regime in South Africa, even though the churches were mostly polarized between the two sides of the conflict, at least until the last few years of the regime, when the Dutch Reformed Church reversed its position on apartheid.

- Third, *economic development*. The basic text on the relation of religion and economic development is, of course, the German sociologist Max Weber's 1905 work *The Protestant Ethic and the Spirit of Capitalism*. Scholars have been arguing over the thesis of this book for over ninety years. However one comes out on this (I happen to be an unreconstructed Weberian), it is clear that some values foster modern economic development more than others. Something *like* Weber's "Protestant ethic" is probably functional in an early phase of capitalist growth—an ethic, whether religiously inspired or not, that values personal discipline, hard work, frugality, and a respect for learning. The new Evangelicalism in Latin America exhibits these values in virtually crystalline purity, so that my own mental subtitle for the research project on this topic conducted by the center I direct at Boston University has been, "Max Weber is alive and well and living in Guatemala." Conversely, Iberian Catholicism, as it was established in Latin America, clearly does *not* foster such values.

But religious traditions can change. Spain experienced a remarkably successful period of economic development beginning in the waning years of the Franco regime, and one of the important factors was the influence of the Opus Dei, which combined rigorous theological orthodoxy with a market-friendly openness in economic matters. I have suggested that Islam, by and large, has difficulties with a modern market economy; yet Muslim emigrants have done remarkably well in a number of countries (for instance, in sub-Saharan Africa) and there is a powerful Islamic movement in Indonesia that might yet play a role analogous to that of Opus Dei in the Catholic world. I should add that for years now there has been an extended debate over the part played by Confucian-inspired values in the economic success stories of East Asia; if one is to credit the "post-Confucian thesis" and also to allow that Confucianism is a religion, then here would be a very important religious contribution to economic development.

One morally troubling aspect of this matter is that values functional at one period of economic development may not be functional at another. The values of the "Protestant ethic" or a functional equivalent thereof are probably essential during the phase that Walt Rostow called "the take-off," but may not be so in a later phase. Much less austere values may be more functional in the so-called post-industrial economies of Europe, North America, and East Asia. For example, frugality, however admirable from a moral viewpoint may actually be a vice economically speaking. Although undisciplined hedonists have a hard time climbing out of primitive poverty, they can do well in the high-tech, knowledge-driven economies of the advanced societies.

- Finally, *human rights and social justice*. Religious institutions have, of course, made many statements on human rights and social justice. Some of these have had important political consequences, as in the civil-rights struggle in the United States and the collapse of Communist regimes in Europe. But, as mentioned previously, there are different religiously articulated views about the nature of human rights. The same goes for ideas about social justice: what is justice to some groups is gross injustice to others. Sometimes it is very clear that positions taken by religious groups on such matters are based on a religious rationale; the principled opposition to abortion and contraception by the Roman Catholic Church is such a clear case. At other times, though, positions on social justice, even if legitimated by religious rhetoric, reflect the location of the religious functionaries in this or that network of non-religious social classes and interests. To stay with the same example, I think that this is the case with most of the positions taken by American Catholic institutions on social justice issues other than those relating to sexuality and reproduction.

I have dealt very briefly with immensely complex matters. I was asked to give a global overview, and that is what I have tried to do. There is no way that I can end this with some sort of uplifting sermon. Both those who have great hopes for the role of religion in the affairs of this world and those who *fear* this role must be disappointed by the factual evidence. In assessing this role, there is no alternative to a nuanced, case-by-case approach. But one statement can be made with great confidence: Those who neglect religion in their analyses of contemporary affairs do so at great peril.

Roman Catholicism in the Age of John Paul II

George Weigel

On the edge of the twenty-first century, the impact of the Roman Catholic Church on world affairs vividly illustrates what Professor Peter Berger described as the nonsecularization of late modernity. That Catholic impact, which can be measured empirically from Manila to Kraków, and from Santiago de Chile to Seoul, also refutes the expectations—indeed, the deeply cherished hopes—of many of the founding fathers of the modern world.

Voltaire, it will be remembered, died with the wish that the last king be strangled with the guts of the last priest, and the revolution he helped to inspire defined its goal as little less than the overthrow of the civilization the Church had helped nurture for centuries. When Italian troops occupied Rome in 1870, completed the unification of Italy by absorbing the Papal States, and sent the pope into internal exile as the "prisoner of the Vatican," it was widely thought that the Catholic Church was a spent historical force. As recently as 1919, only twenty-six states, mainly from Latin America, maintained diplomatic representation at the Holy See, and the Vatican was blocked (by Clause 15 of the secret accord that bound Italy to the Allies in 1915) from participating in the Versailles Peace Conference.

The view today is rather different. Roman Catholicism is now a vastly complex religious community of one billion adherents, more than 17 per cent of the world's population, living in virtually every country on the planet. Its membership shows a dazzling diversity: Helmut Kohl and Jacques Chirac, Henry Hyde and Daniel Patrick Moynihan, Mel Gibson and Martin Sheen, Mother Teresa and Lech Walesa, Princess Michael of Kent and Cherie (Mrs. Tony) Blair, New York Yankees manager Joe Torre and New York philanthropist Lew Lehrman, composer Henryk Górecki and "Cranberries" lead singer Dolores O'Riordan.

From *The Desecularization of the World: Resurgent Religion and World Politics*, Edited by Peter Berger, pp. 19–35. Copyright © 1999 by Wm. B. Eerdmans Publishing Co. Reprinted by permission of Wm. B. Eerdmans Publishing Co.

That community of faith, worship, and charity is served by some 4,300 bishops, 404,500 priests, 848,500 women religious, and 428,000 mission catechists, who are organized into 2,842 dioceses located in venues as various as New York City, São Salvador di Bahia, Samoa-Apia, Paris, Prague, Bombay, and Kinshasa. The Church sponsors some 172,800 educational institutions around the world (running the gamut from simple village preschools to distinguished research universities) and operates some 105,100 social-welfare institutions—hospitals, dispensaries, and clinics, homes for the old, ill, and handicapped, orphanages, nurseries, and marriage counseling centers. In Third World settings, those institutions are sometimes a region's sole lifeline to modern education and medicine.

Today, 166 states exchange full diplomatic representation with the Holy See, a unique entity recognized in international law as the juridical embodiment of the universal ministry of the Bishop of Rome as the head of the Roman Catholic Church. In addition to these bilateral relations, the Holy See also maintains diplomatic representation at regional organizations like the Organization on Security and Co-operation in Europe and the Organization of American States. Holy See representatives have served in recent years as mediators of border disputes (notably in securing the Beagle Channel boundary agreement between Chile and Argentina); and under Vatican influence, Catholic lay movements like the Rome-based Sant' Egidio Community have played important roles in "third-track diplomacy," most successfully in Mozambique. In addition, the Holy See enters into treaties (known as "concordats") with sovereign states, in order to regulate the religious, educational, and charitable activities of the Church in individual countries, and is a signatory of such international agreements as the Nuclear Non-Proliferation Treaty and the Nuclear Test-Ban Treaty. No one, of course, worried that the colorfully clad Swiss Guards who maintain security at the entrances to the 109-acre Vatican compound in Rome might test or acquire nuclear weapons; but the Holy See's participation in such international legal instruments is empirical testimony to the distinctive place it occupies in the formal, legal aspects of international public life, and to the permanence of moral issues in world politics.

Furthermore, it is now widely recognized that the Catholic Church in general, and Pope John Paul II in particular, played indispensable roles in what we have come to know as the Revolution of 1989 in east central Europe. The terms in which the Pope and the Church helped to bring about the demise of European Communism remain controverted. But that John Paul II was a key figure, and perhaps *the* key figure, in the drama of the 1980s is now conceded by Mikhail Gorbachev and Carl Bernstein, if not by the editors of *The New York Times* and *Foreign Affairs*. In a similar vein, and within roughly the same time-frame, one could also note the role played by Catholic clergy, religious, and lay leaders in the non-violent resistance to the Pinochet regime in Chile, in various other democratic transitions in Central and South America, in the overthrow of the Marcos regime in the Philippines, and in the democratization of South Korea. Voltaire must be spinning in his grave.

The Evangelical Upsurge

David Martin

. . . I have tried to characterize the Evangelical upsurge around the world, particularly in its social and political manifestations, and to give some examples of the varied forms it has taken. In this section I will pick up some themes that bear on its future.

In his essay in this book, Peter Berger makes the point that the vitality of conservative religious groups in all three major monotheistic faiths is cognate with the relative decline of liberal groups that have attempted to conform to "modernity as defined by progressive intellectuals." At the same time, the major attempts in this century to institute what T. S. Eliot called "the idea of a Christian society" have all gone into decline. The Neo-Calvinist movement to constitute a specifically Christian culture was never very effective, whatever its intellectual underpinnings. Liberation theology was more effective in the proposals of its intellectual protagonists than in everyday reality, and it has declined since the arrival of Pope John Paul II and the passing of the Latin American political crises of the 1960s and 1970s. Christian Democracy always had a strong admixture of secularizing dynamism and is now, with the evanescence of dogmatic Communism, chronically lacking a plausible antagonist. This means that within societies with a Christian tradition, even in such strongly religious countries as the Irish Republic and Poland, the old inclusive frame allied to ecclesiastical monopoly is no longer viable. The Roman Catholic Church, even in Italy, accepts the fact that it cannot hope to dominate a society through a party such as "Democrazia Cristiana," and therefore sees itself as a potent commentator within a pluralistic framework, possessed at the same time of concrete institutional interests.

That role, the role of influential commentator within a pluralistic society, still exists, and it is probably the one that will eventually be taken up by the expanding Evangelical movements of the contemporary

From *The Desecularization of the World: Resurgent Religion and World Politics*, Edited by Peter Berger, pp. 48–49. Copyright © 1999 by Wm. B. Eerdmans Publishing Co. Reprinted by permission from Wm. B. Eerdmans Publishing Co.

world. True, sometimes those movements are drawn by the cultural pull of societies in which they operate to adopt corporatist models of intervention; sometimes they even entertain notions of replacing the Catholic Church in its old domination of public space. But that remains a dream. The likelihood is that Evangelicals will work within parties as commentators on the moral condition of society. In that respect Evangelical movements will exhibit a powerful contrast with those Islamic movements that seek the regulation of a whole society according to religious norms.

The Evangelicals' most potent contribution will be the creation of voluntary associations and the multiplication of social and political actors in the public arena. Other things being equal (which of course they rarely are), the cultural characteristics of Evangelicals—participation, pragmatism, competition, personal discipline—ought in the long run to foster democracy.

Political Islam

Abdullahi A. An-Na'im

. . . As a matter of historical fact . . . the relationship between Islam and politics was never premised on the so-called Islamic state or the comprehensive application of *Shari'a*. True, ruling elites have usually sought Islamic legitimacy for their political power, but that can hardly define an "Islamic state" as a clear model that can be implemented today. Similarly, *Shari'a* always had its role in the life of Muslim individuals and communities, but that was by way of personal commitment and voluntary practice, rather than through coercive enforcement by the organs of the state.[1]

The notion of an "Islamic state" is an innovation developed by fundamentalists during the second half of the twentieth century. It is inherently inconsistent with the obvious fact that the divine sources of Islam cannot be understood and applied except through human reason and the concrete experience of Muslim societies. Since the outcome is necessarily a mixture of divine guidance and the human endeavor to understand and benefit from it, the institution that emerges from that combination is not a theocratic state; it is, rather, a human attempt to apply religious values to political, social, and economic affairs. Given the inevitable change in human affairs, especially in the modern world, a state that is informed by Islamic values must constantly evolve and adapt to new circumstances.[2] To call such a state "Islamic" is misleading because it contradicts the reality of the great diversity of Islamic religious and political thought; it is an attempt to monopolize religious legitimacy for a particular and necessarily limited human conception. . . .

. . . there is no escape from human agency in the conduct of the affairs of any society. In the case of Islamic societies, human agency is unavoidable in the interpretation of the Qur'an and Sunna, as well as in the development and implementation of state policies. Where the inherent fallibility of this unavoidable human agency is openly

From *The Desecularization of the World: Resurgent Religion and World Politics*, Edited by Peter Berger, pp. 116–117. Copyright © 1999 by Wm. B. Eerdmans Publishing Co. Reprinted by permission from Wm. B. Eerdmans Publishing Co.

acknowledged, there will be opportunities for peaceful disagreement that can be regulated through appropriate political and legal institutions. That possibility is lost, however, when the reality of human agency is denied or disguised as an Islamic state applying divine Shari'a.

An Islamic vs. a European Approach to Secularism

In response to fundamentalist demands, many Muslim intellectuals today tend to advocate European conceptions of strict separation between Islam and political authority, legislation, and the administration of justice. This approach, which I will call secularism, is unlikely to succeed, because it fails to address the issue of its cultural legitimacy for the Muslim state. In particular, without addressing fundamentalist claims that they are seeking the establishment of an Islamic state to implement *Shari'a,* advocates of secularism will appear to be calling on their own societies to abandon their Islamic cultural and religious foundations in order to adopt philosophical models that have emerged from European experiences with Christianity and the Enlightenment. In practical political terms, moreover, secularism is untenable in Islamic societies, not only because it does not represent religious and cultural values, but also because it came to Islamic societies in the dubious company of Western colonialism and post-colonial hegemony.

Advocates of secularism for Islamic societies are clearly motivated by objections to the agenda of Islamic fundamentalists; they fear the disastrous consequences of that form of political Islam for national politics and international relations. Ironically, however, their advocacy of secularism may in fact strengthen what they are opposing. If presented with European secularism as the only alternative to the so-called Islamic state and application of *Shari'a,* Islamic societies will clearly prefer the latter, however serious its conceptual faults and practical difficulties. Clear illustration of the risks of strict secularism can be seen in Iran in the drastic reversal since 1979 of every "secular" achievement of the previous regime, and in the fact that the Turkish army is the primary guardian of secularism more than seventy years after Atatürk's authoritarian effort to radically reformulate the Turkish state and society.[3] It is clear that in this age of self-determination, democracy, and the protection of human rights as a matter of international law, secularism cannot be forced on any Islamic society by an authoritarian regime. Whenever Islamic societies exercise their right to self-determination by

36

choosing their own system of government, the outcome is unlikely to favor European conceptions of secularism.

In light of all this, I conclude that what must be done is to clarify and specify the relationship between Islam and political authority on the basis of an Islamic approach to secularism. Such an approach requires the best possible opportunities for public discourse and experimentation over time, in light of scholarly research to extrapolate the essence of Islamic values from the historical circumstances of early Islamic societies. From this perspective, the protection of basic human rights, especially freedom of belief, expression, and association, is an Islamic imperative—and not merely a requirement of international treaties—because these rights are prerequisites for the necessary discourse. The crucial safeguard throughout this process, as well as during the implementation of whatever models may emerge, is strict observance of the principle of pluralism and the protection of human rights.

Endnotes

[1] Lapidus, *History of Islamic Societies*, 120–125.

[2] Ali Abd-al-Raziq, al-Islam wa usul al-Hukm (Arabic) (Cairo: Matbatt Misr, 1925); Abdelwahab El-Affendi, *Who Needs an Islamic State?*, 117. (London: Grey Seal Books, 1991).

[3] Joel Beinin and Joe Stork, *Political Islam*, Chapter 12. (Los Angeles: University of California Press, 1990).

A Liberal Democracy and the Fate of the Earth

J. Ronald Engel

. . . Of all the reasons that might be given for our failure, I believe there is only one, finally, that goes to the root of the matter: it is a failure of faith. This was Vaclav Havel's message to the United States Congress in February of 1990.

While acknowledging that Eastern Europe has much to learn from the West about free elections and free markets, he insisted that the West also has much to learn from the East: "a special capacity to look, from time to time, somewhat further than someone who has not undergone [our] bitter experience."[1]

Havel then spelled out what the West had to learn: that it is a long way from realizing the ideal of democracy, that it is "still under the sway of the destructive and vain belief that man is the pinnacle of creation, and not just a part of it, and that therefore everything is permitted," that it has yet to understand that the salvation of the world lies in a "global revolution in human consciousness," not in economic growth, that the locus of this transformation is the conscience of each and every citizen, worker as well as intellectual, and that this is so because conscience is the mediator of our responsibility to "the order of Being."[2]

What Havel in effect told the American people was that they have lost their faith; and he concluded by noting that what they have lost is of no small moment in world history. For their faith wrote the Declaration of Independence, the Bill of Rights, and the Constitution, and it still has power to "inspire us to be citizens." Havel was retrieving the faith of the eighteenth-century democratic revolutions when such phrases as "we the people," "consent of the governed," "freedom of conscience," "inalienable rights," and "the laws of nature and Nature's God" were living and self-evident truths.

This was the faith that many in Eastern Europe rediscovered in their "bitter experience" since the Second Great War, and it is the truth they now have to share with the rest of the world.

It is striking that the slogan of the Czechoslovakian revolution was the Hussite conviction, "the truth shall prevail"; [sic] that these are the words Thomas Jefferson echoed when he wrote in the "Act for Establishing Religious Freedom in Virginia": "that truth which is universal is great," and if left to herself, "will prevail"; and that when Havel tried to put his finger on the spiritual center of the Czechoslovakian revolution he used the phrase, "living in the truth."

Havel explains the meaning of "living in the truth" in his essay, "Politics and Conscience." He opens with a personal experience:

> As a boy, I lived for some time in the country and I clearly remembered an experience from those days: I used to walk to school in a nearby village along a cart track through the fields and, on the way, see on the horizon a huge smokestack of some hurriedly built factory, in all likelihood in the service of war. It spewed dense brown smoke and scattered it across the sky. Each time I saw it, I had an intense sense of something profoundly wrong, of humans soiling the heavens. I have no idea whether there was something like a science of ecology in those days; if there was, I certainly knew nothing of it. Still that "soiling the heavens" offended me spontaneously. It seemed to me that, in it, humans are guilty of something, that they destroy something important, arbitrarily disrupting the natural order of things, and that such things cannot go unpunished.[3]

Interpreting this event, Havel says that the sense of good and evil he so strongly felt that day was his personal experience of the Absolute. It was an experience of a reality that youth takes [sic] for granted but from which most modern adults are alienated.

. . . Sometimes it is said that the liberal democratic faith does not require belief in God; one may be "anything one chooses," an atheist, a humanist, a theist. This is true if by it we mean that no *particular* idea of God is required, but far from true if we mean that no higher order or authority, no Absolute is presupposed in human experience. As Thoreau wrote, "This is the only way, we say; but there are as many ways as there can be drawn radii from one center."[4]

This, however, is a minimal understanding of the liberal democratic faith. The real God of liberal democracy is a God of overflowing fertility, growth, plenitude, and abundance. It is what Havel tries to describe when he writes: "Life rebels against all uniformity and leveling; its aim is not sameness, but variety, the restlessness of transcendence, the adventure of novelty and rebellion against the status quo. An essential condition of its enhancement is the secret constantly made manifest."[5] And it is what Thoreau also tried to describe when he wrote: "I see, smell, taste, hear, feel, that everlasting Something to which we are allied, at once our maker, our abode, our destiny, our very Selves . . . the actual glory of the universe."[6]

Since no individual, indeed, no people, will ever experience more than an infinitesimal part of this glory, each person and each religion should be eager to learn from every other, and to engage in the most precious ritual in the religion of democracy, public dialogue and mutual persuasion.

The Truth Shall *Prevail!*

To awaken to the liberal democratic faith is to awaken to Spirit in Nature. It is to become a political and ecological revolutionary. For if we hold this faith, "we the people" have grounds to trust the ultimate identity between our spirits and the Absolute Spirit, and this means we have grounds to think for ourselves, to trust our own experience, to trust one another, to trust the world, to believe that what we find good will be preserved in the order of things. And this means *all* of us, including the *least* of us, and it means *all* of nature, including the *least thing* in nature.

To lose this faith is to cut the nerve of liberal democracy, to remove the motivation to live responsibly under the difficult, often tragic, conditions of life as it is given to us. In Thoreau's judgment, "It is hard to be a good citizen of the world in any *great* sense. . . ."[7] To doubt that Spirit infuses Nature is to doubt that citizenship is possible. It is to reduce personal experience and responsibility to an absurdity. It is to lapse into a world of isolated selves and to sever human experience from nature.

Havel believes that the reason we have failed to carry forward the revolutionary promise of liberal democracy is that we have betrayed this faith. In effect, we have violated the common ground of our being.

We must then forgive one another and renew the covenant. For the fate of the earth depends on our reconstituting the natural world as the true terrain of citizenship. This means pledging ourselves, in Havel's words, to

> . . . draw our standards from our natural world, heedless of ridicule, and reaffirm its denied validity. We must honour with the humility of the wise the

41

bounds of that natural world and the mystery which lies beyond them, admitting that there is something in the order of being which evidently exceeds all our competence; relating ever again to the absolute horizon of our existence which, if we but will, we shall constantly discover and experience.[8]

This is why, he concludes, our hope lies with those "single, seemingly powerless" persons who dare "to cry out the word of truth and to stand behind it."[9]

Endnotes

[1] Havel, "Help the Soviet Union on its Road to Democracy," 330.

[2] Ibid.

[3] Havel, *Living the Truth*, 136.

[4] Henry David Thoreau, *Walden*, ed. J. Lyndon Shanley (Princeton, NJ: Princeton University Press, 1983), 173–174.

[5] Havel, *Living the Truth*, 23.

[6] Henry David Thoreau, *The Illustrated a Week on the Concord and Merrimack Rivers*, ed. Carl Hovde, William Howarth, and Elizabeth Witherell (Princeton: Princeton University Press, 1983), 173–174.

[7] Henry David Thoreau, *Journal of Henry D. Thoreau*, ed. Bradford Torrey and Francis H. Allen (New York: Dover Publications, 1962), vol. 1, 106. Emphasis added.

[8] Havel, *Living the Truth*, 153.

[9] Ibid., 156.

When Religion Becomes Evil

Charles Kimball

Our awareness of the complexities and dangers of global conflicts has grown significantly since the sobering events of September 11, 2001. Our knowledge concerning the causes and possible solutions to these conflicts lags behind, but we are learning important new lessons each day. We know that religion remains one of the most powerful forces in human society and that religious ideologies and commitments are often directly linked with violent conflict. We know with certainty that well-organized groups of motivated people are capable of wreaking havoc on a global scale. At the beginning of this book, I offered the edge of a cliff as a metaphor for the precarious place where we find ourselves standing today and suggested that progress is best defined as taking one step back. This book represents an effort to step back, by identifying clearly the major warning signs of corruption in religion that invariably lead to violence and evil in the world.

The complicity of religious persuasions in global conflicts today is undeniable, but understanding this complicity requires that we clearly grasp the difference between what we have called corrupt forms of religious commitment and the authentic forms that offer hope. Throughout much of the book we have described the five telltale signs of corruption in religion.* As we have seen, one or more of these five signs always precedes any instance of religiously sanctioned evil. Knowledge of such corruption is invaluable in today's world, yet it is not sufficient in itself. Whether one is a true believer or a die-hard secularist, it remains necessary to take the next step from the knowledge of these factors that predict *when religion becomes evil* to a clear understanding of *how religion can remain true to its authentic sources* and a force for positive change.

*Kimball defines these signs as:
1) Absolute Truth Claims; 2) Blind Obedience; 3) Establishing the "Ideal" time; 4) The End Justifies Any Means; 5) Declaring Holy War.

As we have explored each of the warning signs of corrupted religion, we have seen how correctives were always present within each tradition. Our study of the pathological has helped to elucidate the healthy. At the heart of every major religious tradition we find abiding truths and principles that provide the first antidote to violence and extremism. It is important to recall that violent extremists are on the fringe of these traditions for a reason: the large majority of adherents recognize that the extremists violate the most basic teachings and values within the tradition. But as our examples have shown, many sincere people are susceptible to authoritative claims made by charismatic leaders. It is all too easy to lose sight of the most basic teachings in one's religion, particularly when oppressive social, political, or economic conditions figure prominently into the arguments advanced and sacred texts quoted by authoritative claims made by charismatic leaders. Fear, insecurity, and a desire to protect the status quo can foster a tribalism in which otherwise sincere people engage in dehumanizing patterns of behavior, even war.

Nevertheless, in my view, people of faith offer the best hope both for correcting the corruptions leading to violence and for leading the way into a more promising future. At the outset, we affirmed that religious ideas and commitments have inspired individuals and communities of faith to transcend narrow self-interest in pursuit of higher values and truths. Throughout history religion has often been connected with what is noblest and best in human beings. Now, perhaps more than ever, religious people must transcend narrowly defined self-interest and seek new ways to live out what is noblest and best in their faith traditions.

We have seen truths common to each of the major religious traditions. These same traditions that have nurtured millions of people have also inspired adherents to rediscover, redefine in contemporary terms, and deepen these truths amid changing circumstances over the centuries. Such an impetus for reform is urgently needed today. All the resources needed for reform can be found at the heart of the major religious traditions. Even in the face of the worst examples of religious extremism, a strong and clear voice for change always sounds from the center of those traditions. Scott Appleby, who coedited the five-volume *Fundamentalism Project* with Martin Marty, has been studying religious extremism for more than a decade.[1] Appleby argues convincingly that deeply committed religious peacemakers provide a major source of hope. He, too, suggests the respective religious traditions can once again serve us well.

The religious tradition is a vast and complex body of wisdom built up over many generations. Its foundational sources—sacred scriptures and/or codified oral teachings and commentaries—express and interpret the experiences of the sacred that led to the formation of the religious community. A religious tradition is no less than these sources, but it is always more. The deeper meaning and significance of these sources continues to be revealed throughout history. In each of the major religious traditions of the world, prophets, theologians, sages, scholars, and simple believers, exalted by the holy lives they led, refined and deepened the tradition's spiritual practices and theological teachings in support of peacemaking rather than war, reconciliation rather than retaliation. To be traditional, then, is to take seriously those developments that achieved authoritative status because they probed, clarified, and developed the insights and teachings contained in the foundational sources.[2]

Pursuing Peace with Justice

We look back in order to learn how to best move forward. This much is crystal clear: holy war is not holy. However deep the grievances and perceived injustices may be, holy war is not the answer. Whatever religious justifications Christians or Muslims put forward in the past, the results of "holy" warfare were consistently catastrophic. To pursue holy war today is to rush headlong down a dead-end street. Healthy religion speaks not of war but the promise of peace with justice. People of faith, today more than ever, must look deep into their traditions for clarity and guidance about the paths that will lead toward peace and justice.

Some extreme circumstances may call for military force, but we must all be wary when political leaders seek to justify policies on religious grounds. The multiple dynamics and continuing fallout from the Gulf War stand as a powerful reminder that military action must, at the very least, meet the high standards of just war criteria. But even this is highly dubious. Given the nature of modern weapons and the dangerous ways regional conflicts can ignite a wider conflagration, Christian and Muslim versions of just war criteria may no longer be applicable.

The only intelligent way forward is the route laid out by authentic religion: we must be peacemakers. Yet working for peace and justice is exceedingly difficult. Passivity, isolationism, wishful thinking, or holding hands, lighting candles, and singing "We Are the World" may provide an illusion of peace, but hard work in the dense thicket of the particulars is required. We must try to understand and address those factors that lead to holy war. The religious communities—Christian and Muslims in particular—can lead the way by affirming the promise

45

of peace in their respective traditions and committing themselves to nonviolent resolution of conflict.

For Christians, the historic peace churches and well-established groups within various denominations have been working diligently to develop resources and models for ministries of reconciliation. A relatively new and promising initiative among Christian ethicists, theologians, and experts in conflict resolution has produced an alternative to pacifism and just war theory: the just peacemaking paradigm. In this paradigm the focus shifts to initiatives that can help prevent war and foster peace. Working during the 1990s, the scholars and activists developed ten key practices and detailed guidelines for peacemaking:

1. Support nonviolent direct action.
2. Take independent initiatives to reduce threat.
3. Use cooperative conflict resolution.
4. Acknowledge responsibility for conflict and injustice and seek repentance and forgiveness.
5. Advance democracy, human rights, and religious liberty.
6. Foster just and sustainable economic development.
7. Work with emerging cooperative forces in the international system.
8. Strengthen the United Nations and international efforts for cooperation and human rights.
9. Reduce offensive weapons and weapons trade.
10. Encourage grassroots peacemaking groups and voluntary associations.[3]

Jews, Muslims, and Christians with particular concern for peace and justice in the Middle East can find many groups and resources working strenuously for peace.[4] The casual observer may conclude that peace with justice is not possible in the Middle East, but many people in all three communities have been striving and will continue to strive for the only future that can work, a shared future. The long-standing Israeli-Palestinian conflict defies simple solutions. If the past teaches us anything, however, it is that peace, justice, and security cannot be achieved and maintained through violent means. A Palestinian Jew two thousand years ago warned that violence begets violence and that "those who live by the sword will perish by the sword."

For Muslims, the challenge is most formidable. Many Muslim individuals and groups have clearly rejected the military meaning of *jihad*, most notably Sufis, who have emphasized its spiritual meaning. But these have been more the exception than the rule. For most

Muslims, the military dimensions of *jihad* have been a legitimate feature of their religious tradition. The religious and political dynamics in the world today require Muslims of goodwill to place their emphasis—personally and publicly—on "greater *jihad*," the struggle with the self and the good works of the heart, hands, and tongue for the betterment of society. In the face of those who would wage holy war in the name of Islam, Muslims who embrace their religion as a religion of peace must find the resources to live out the call for peace and justice in society.

Raymond of Agiles's grim description of the crusaders' attack on Jerusalem amounted, in his words, to "small matters" in comparison with what he didn't report. The unspeakable horror perpetrated by "holy" warriors at the portico of Solomon on the Temple Mount defied "powers of belief." The attacks on September 11 are the modern-day parallel to his description. The potential use of chemical, biological, or nuclear weapons by self-proclaimed zealous warriors for God or in response to them tests our "powers of belief." Grave dangers facing the world community demand focused, intentional, and persistent "striving" together for peace and justice.

Pluralism

Advocates of a pluralist position see Christianity neither as the only means to salvation nor as the fulfillment of other religious traditions. The pluralist position affirms the viability of various paths. John Hick, perhaps the most prominent advocate of this approach, called for a "Copernican revolution" in theological thinking thirty years ago. Extending the analogy from astronomy, Hick argued for a theocentric approach, a "shift from the dogma that Christianity is at the centre to the realisation that it is God who is at the centre, and that all religions . . . serve and revolve around him." Hick develops his theocentric position in his book *God Has Many Names*. Hick argues that the world's religious traditions are best understood as "different response to the one divine Reality." The distinctions among religious communities, in his view, arise largely through perceptions conditioned by historical and cultural circumstances.[5]

Wilfred Cantwell Smith articulated a more radical approach to pluralism in his book *Towards a World Theology*. Smith was suspicious of any Christian theological framework that maintained a "we-they" interpretation from within a boundaried and self-sufficient Christian position looking out over other communities of faith as objects or even people upon whom to make pronouncements, however generous." He attempted—and encouraged Christians, Muslims, Hindus, Jews, Buddhists, Sikhs, and others to attempt—something grander: "to interpret intellectually all human faith, one's own and others', comprehensively and justly."[6]

Harvey Cox's popular book *Many Mansions* facilitated a discussion of religious pluralism among local clergy and people in the pews.[7] The title of his book is taken from the King James translation of John 14:2: "In my Father's house there are many mansions; if it were not so I would have told you." Cox's pluralist approach invites people to gather for mutually enriching dialogue. Diana Eck, whose extraordinary leadership in documenting the religious landscape in the United States at the turn of the millennium led President Clinton to award her with a National Humanities Medal in 1998, identifies herself as a "Christian pluralist":

> Through the years I have found my own faith not threatened, but broadened and deepened by the study of Hindu, Buddhist, Muslim, and Sikh traditions of faith. And I have found that only as a Christian pluralist could I be faithful to the mystery and the presence of the one I call God. Being a Christian pluralist means daring to encounter people of different faith traditions and defining my faith not by its borders but by its roots.[8]

Eck's theological outlook has been shaped both by the study of other religious traditions and by her personal encounter with Hindus, Muslims, Buddhists, Jews, Sikhs, and others.[9] Her first in-depth experience of another major religious tradition came in college during an extended visit to India. For Eck, the personal encounter with pious, practicing Hindus challenged many presuppositions related to her upbringing as a Methodist in Montana. Personal encounter is often the catalyst for an inner dialogue that prompts theological reflection on religious diversity. For me, the process began with a Jewish grandfather and extended family. Personal experience and dialogue with those of other faiths are common denominators for many Western Christians who study world religions and try to articulate a coherent theology of pluralism. For people in many parts of the world, of course, self-conscious awareness of religious diversity is not new; dialogical encounter has been a way of life for centuries.

John Hick, Wilfred Smith, Huston Smith, Harvey Cox, Diana Eck, and a host of other scholars have stimulated widespread reflection on issues of particularity and pluralism. For two decades Christian self-understanding in the midst of religious diversity has been at the center of serious theological debate.[10] The discussion has been lively also among lay Christians. During the past quarter century, I have traveled throughout the United States speaking on college campuses, in churches, and at conferences on issues related to the Middle East, Islam, and Jewish-Christian-Muslim relations. Almost without exception, people want to talk about how they view Christianity amid the multiplicity of religions. I have often found that nonspecialists are well ahead of Christian leaders in being willing to explore with an open mind the ideas and practices in other religions. These people are often developing their reflection in the context of a religiously mixed marriage or through friendship with a Jewish neighbor or a Hindu co-worker.

Nothing approaching consensus is taking shape as various forms of exclusivist, inclusivist, and pluralist paradigms are presented, dissected, and critiqued. In my view, each position has value. When I am asked about my own views on these matters, I sometimes respond like my former college professor: "What I think is not what is important for you. What do *you* think? And, more importantly, what do you feel *you* should *do* as a responsible Christian (or Muslim or Jew) in your religiously diverse neighborhood and interdependent world community?" I respond this way at times because some people want an authority figure to provide simple answers for them. We all have to think and be responsible for ourselves. Sometimes it is clear that a questioner wants to put me (or whomever) into a category he or she deems heretical in order to justify dismissing all that has been said. I've always been puzzled and saddened by people who make clear they couldn't be very happy in heaven unless hell was full to overflowing with people who disagree with their particularly theology.

I am a Christian and a member of the clergy. My study, teaching, writing, and ecumenical ministry in the Middle East are all connected to a strong sense of vocation. I have learned a great deal from and been immeasurably enriched by people whose religious traditions—or deep skepticism about religion—provide a distinctly different worldview. But in my study and experience, I have yet to discover truths that compel me to embrace another religious tradition as my own. My olive tree has deep roots. Like Diana Eck, I have found that the powerful truths and spiritual discipline I've seen among Jews, Muslims, Hindus, and others has often opened my eyes to dimensions of the Christian tradition that previously had been obscured or unknown to me. At the same time, I know many Muslims, Hindus, Jews, Buddhists, and others who not only say the same thing about their religious tradition with sincerity and conviction but visibly live out their faith in compassionate service for others. Experience makes plain that my experience of God, my human view of truth, does not begin to exhaust the possibilities.

What I find most encouraging in the serious, ongoing debates and personal investigations is that none of the options necessarily precludes positive, cooperative engagement with people of other traditions on common problems facing our communities, our nations, and our world. Working together for the common good must be a major focus of interfaith dialogue in the years ahead. Christians and Muslims, for example, do not need to come to theological agreement before they can work hand in hand to meet the needs of the poor in their community or address such issues as equitable public education or the proliferation of drugs in society. When people from different faith traditions get to know one another, they often discover quickly that they have a great deal in common, particularly in terms of what their faith requires in relation to their neighbors. Whatever one's theology, it should be shaped both by the wisdom of time-tested sources such as scripture and tradition and in the context of new information as well as contemporary life experiences.

At the conclusion of *Many Mansions*, Harvey Cox issues a call to action, arguing that the future is now in our hands because God has placed it there.

> Thus, the possibility of self-annihilation requires us to put all our questions not in the form, What will happen? but rather in the form, What must we do? . . . As time-bound creatures, we must work with the stubborn stuff of past and present. Among the "givens" are our existing religious traditions, which, far from dying out, appear to be leaping into a period of resurgence. But neither can we wait for kismet to deliver us into a new era in which we no longer need to project our inmost terrors onto the heavens or onto other peoples and nations. We must now take the initiative, not just to predict the future—including the future of religion—but to shape it.[11]

Cox's call to action, to take the initiative to shape the future, resonates with the approach I have advocated throughout this book. Nowhere is the call to action more needed today than in the Middle East.

The Middle East as a Microcosm

When Abraham packed up his family and belongings, the Genesis story tells us, he looked toward a promised land with the assurance that God's blessing would extend through him to all the people on earth.

Today, nearly half the world's population traces its spiritual heritage back to Abraham. While Jews, Christians, and Muslims share a claim in God's blessing, the everyday reality has often been disturbingly different. Time and again we have seen violent and destructive behavior by Christians, Muslims, and Jews. Many of the most volatile and dangerous religious corruptions today are directly connected to the Middle East—most visibly, though not exclusively, to the Arab-Israeli-Palestinian conflict. The dynamics in Israel/Palestine represent a kind of microcosm for the world community. If we are not able to find non-violent ways to move forward toward justice, peace, and security in these lands, it does not bode well for the rest of us inhabiting the religiously diverse, interdependent world community.

As I said in the previous chapter, people in the United States bear a particular responsibility. We are citizens in the democratic nation that is also the world's superpower, and we are responsible for what is said and done in our name. Unlike the government of Sri Lanka or Sweden, the U.S. government has a profound and daily impact on the lives of people in the Middle East and elsewhere. "We the people" are represented by this government. Those who declare the Middle East conflict is too complicated or who justify noninvolvement by saying "those people have always fought and always will" are being irresponsible as citizens and, if they claim a religious identity, as people of faith. Christians are called to a pastoral, prophetic, and reconciling ministry in the world. As William Sloane Coffin reminds us, Jesus' teachings and the writings of Paul are to be applied precisely where the challenges are greatest. There are no easy answers or simple solutions. But, like Martin Luther King, Jr. or Bishop Desmond Tutu in South Africa, we have a spiritual compass to provide an orientation and the principles on which to base our action.

Jews and Muslims also have a major stake as citizens and as people of faith. Jews are rightly concerned with security and stability for Israel. If the conflicts during much of the past century have taught anything it is that security cannot ultimately be achieved by force. Israel's overwhelming military superiority has not secured the peace. Israel's long-term self-interest is inextricably linked to peace, political stability, and economic prosperity. None of these is possible apart from peace, security, political stability, and economic opportunity for Palestinians. Most Jews I know have a deep attachment to Israel *and* a deep concern for the well-being of others. Both require active pursuit of policies that will facilitate peaceful coexistence in the Middle East.

For Muslims, the Middle East conflict presents an enormous challenge and opportunity. We have identified a number of serious problems contributing to frustration and fostering extremism in certain predominantly Islamic lands. Muslims living in the West must lead the way in calling for a halt to human rights abuses and for new forms of participatory governments, religious freedom, and economic opportunities. While there is no fast track to a healthy future in many countries, violent extremism is clearly not the answer. It is both contradictory to the spirit of Islam and highly counterproductive. Muslims committed to peaceful coexistence and constructive change through nonviolent means must step forward and provide leadership that truly reflects their affirmation that Islam is a religion of peace.

Wishful thinking? Perhaps, but I don't think so. While no one can predict the future, we can learn from the horrific mistakes and corruptions of the past. This is what we must do, in fact, if we hope to enjoy a future together on this planet. Having spent a great deal of my professional life in the midst of Middle East issues, I remain optimistic. Behind the headlines and sinister behavior of people on the extremes can be found the large majority of people in the Middle East—Jews, Muslims, and Christians—who deeply desire peace. People there, like people everywhere, long for a better future for their children and grandchildren. And many individuals and organizations are working actively for political reconciliation and a shared future in the land God promised to Abraham's descendants.[12]

Can we achieve justice and peace in the Middle East? . . . Perfect justice and total peace are beyond our reach, particularly since people define these goals in different terms and through different understandings of truth. But proximate justice and peaceful coexistence are realistic goals for those who avoid the pitfalls of absolute truth claims and who are committed to working toward a better future using means that are consistent with the desired ends. People in various faith traditions must be clear among themselves and with one another: holy war is not an option.

Far from exhausting all the paths toward peace, we have only begun to marshal the positive energies of religious people. Marc Gopin's book, *Holy War, Holy Peace: How Religion Can Bring Peace to the Middle East*, is full of thoughtful and practical ways people can move away from the model of cosmic conflict and toward the model of reconciliation among estranged family members. Scott Appleby's recent work also provides extremely helpful guidance on how religious communities and nongovernmental organizations can lead the way in transforming conflict and helping to bring about reconciliation. There are many options for those who take seriously the call to be peacemakers.[13]

As people of faith look toward the future—in the Middle East and in their own communities—we would all do well to focus on the twofold mandate to love God and to love our neighbor. The Qur'an provides a wise word that celebrates our diversity even as it guides us on the journey of faith, in which our vision and understanding of ultimate truth remain limited: "If God had so willed, He would have created you one community, but He has not done so that He may test you in what He has given you; so compete with one another in good works. To God you shall all return and He will tell you the truth about that which you have been disputing" (Qur'an 5:48).

Endnotes

[1] Martin E. Marty and Scott R. Appleby, eds., *The Fundamentalism Project*, 5 vols. (Chicago: University of Chicago Press, 1991–1995).

[2] R. Scott Appleby, The Ambivalence of the Sacred: Religion, Violence, and Reconciliation (Lanham, MD: Rowman & Littlefield, 2000), 16–17.

[3] Glen Stassen, ed., *Just Peacemaking: Ten Practices for Abolishing War* (New York: Pilgrim Press, 1998).

[4] Numerous remarkable, religiously based organizations are educating and modeling cooperation and coexistence in Israel/Palestine today. The same is true within the United States. One of the more hopeful initiatives in America is the U.S. Interreligious Committee for Peace in the Middle East. This organization, which began in 1986, is made up of more than a thousand Jewish, Christian, and Muslim religious leaders with a common vision for the Middle East. Many avenues are open for peacemaking in one of the most intractable conflicts on Earth. See Marc Gopin, *Holy War, Holy Peace: How Religion Can Bring Peace to the Middle East* (New York: Oxford University Press, 2002), for a thorough and thoughtful series of options that draw upon the resources of the religions.

[5] John Hick, *God Has Many Names*, (London: Macmillan, 1980), 6; Hick, *God and the Universe of Faiths*, (New York: St. Martin's. Press, 1973), 131.

[6] Wilfred Cantwell Smith, *Towards a World Theology: Faith and the Comparative History of Religion.* (Philadelphia: Westminster Press, 1981), 152.

[7] Harvey Cox, *Many Mansions: A Christian's Encounter with Other Faiths.* (Boston: Beacon Press, 1998), 53–57.

[8] Diane L. Eck, *A New Religious America: How a "Christian Country" Has Become the World's Most Religiously Diverse Nation.* (San Francisco: Harper San Francisco, 2001), 23.

[9] See Diana L. Eck, *Encountering God: A Spiritual Journey from Bozeman to Banares* (Boston: Beacon Press, 1993), for a compelling story of her personal pilgrimage—from an active involvement in Methodist youth groups to the scholarly study of world religions and a decade of leadership as the moderator of the World Council of Churches' Subunit on Dialogue with People of Living Faiths.

[10] Many thoughtful works could be cited. The most comprehensive collection of publications and useful bibliographical information is found in the *Faith Meets Faith* series published by Orbis Books. More than forty books have already been published in this collection. Although it is rooted in a Christian theological perspective, the series endorses no single school of thought. Rather, it seeks "to promote interreligious dialogue by providing an open forum for exchanges among followers of different religious paths."

[11] Harvey Cox, *Many Mansions: A Christian's Encounter with Other Faiths*, (Boston: Beacon Press, 1998), 212.

[12] There are literally dozens of groups and organizations working for reconciliation across political and religious lines. Their respective focus and program activities vary from political policies in groups like Peace Now to human rights with *al-haqq* ("the truth," formerly called Law in the Service of Man). Some organizations foster cooperative sports and educational programs. I have worked personally with many different groups, in particular indigenous religious organizations and groups like the American Friends Service Committee and the Mennonite Central Committee. The reconciling ministries of Jews, Muslims, and Christians are often challenged by mistrust arising from violence and extremism, but most people in the region know that their future is interconnected. *New York Times* columnist Tom Friedman captured this sentiment eloquently in an opinion piece on November 21, 2001. He identified Rabbi David Hartman as the kind of "general" needed to fight the "real war," the one taking place in the schools, mosques, churches, and synagogues. Hartman combats religious totalitarianism in Israel by teaching that "God speaks multiple languages and is not exhausted by one faith."

[13] In *Holy War, Holy Peace*, Gopin includes over one hundred pages of "practical applications" for people who are serious in their desire to facilitate peace in the Middle East. See also Scott Appleby's chapters, "Religion and Conflict Resolution," "The Promise of Internal Pluralism: Human Rights and Religious Mission," and "Ambivalence as Opportunity: Strategies for Promoting Religious Peacebuilding" in *Ambivalence of the Sacred*.

Under God?

Michael Perry

It is exceeding unlikely—in any event, there is no evidence to suggest —that religious faith will become a marginal phenomenon among citizens of the United States at any time in the foreseeable future, much less that religious faith in the United States will "wither away."[1]

Although religious faith is not gradually disappearing from the American scene, the religious landscape of the United States is undergoing a significant transformation. In addition to the growing number of religious believers who claim no religious preference, religious faith in the United States is an increasingly diverse phenomenon. Indeed, the United States may well have become, in the last decade, the most religiously diverse nation on earth.[2] "Since the Immigration Act of 1995 eliminated quotas linked to national origin, Muslims, Buddhists, Hindus, Sikhs, Jains, Zoroastrians, and others have arrived in increasing numbers, dramatically altering the religious landscape of many communities. . . . Nationwide, there are now more Buddhists than Presbyterians and nearly as many Muslims as Jews."[3] Given the changing religious landscape of America, those who can bring their religions into the public square face ever more difficult challenges.

That neither the American constitutional idea of nonestablishment nor the morality of liberal democracy calls for marginalizing the role of religious faith in, much less excluding it from, American politics does not mean that religious participation in politics is unproblematic. To bring one's religion to bear as one participates in politics—to rely on religiously grounded moral belief in the course of deliberating about or making political choices—is not necessarily to do so in an inappropriate way. I first addressed the subject of religion in politics in my book *Love and Power*. I sketched there the ideal of "ecumenical politics," which, as I explained, comprised both ecumenical political dialogue and ecumenical political tolerance. As I have noted more than once in this book, I have abandoned the exclusionism I defended in

Love and Power. Nonetheless . . . ecumenical politics still seems to me the right ideal for those in the United States—indeed, in any liberal democracy—who would bring their religion to bear on their politics. The mirror image of ecumenical politics is sectarian politics. Sectarian politics is precisely the wrong ideal.

Consider a mode of religious participation in politics that is bereft of ecumenical generosity—a mode that disdains open-minded engagement with religious views different from one's own and that is little inclined to tolerate ways of life, choices, and acts different from those sanctioned by one's own religious views and conscience. Such a mode of religious participation is not likely to fare well in the increasingly diverse religious environment of the United States. Assume, however, that a sectarian mode of religious participation can sometimes succeed in achieving its political objective(s). Religious believers should nonetheless consider whether what the late Joseph Cardinal Bernardin, archbishop of Chicago, said about his religious community isn't equally applicable to their own: "The Roman Catholic Church should be convinced that we have *much to learn from the world* and much to teach it. A confident church will speak its mind, seek as a community to live its convictions, *but leave space for others to speak to us, to help us grow from their perspective* . . ."[4] Moreover, a sectarian mode of religious participation is more likely, when successful, in achieving its political objective, to tear the bonds of political community than to strengthen them. . . .

For now, we are left with this question: In the years ahead, as this "nation under God" becomes even more religiously diverse, what role will religious faith play, on balance, in our politics? We hope, of course, that it will play a constructive role—even, perhaps, an ennobling role: "Politics that does not contain theology within itself, however little considered, may often be shrewd but remains in the end no more than a business."[5] Hope, however, is not expectation. Many of us will be content if religion plays a role that is not destructive, because we know from history what religion in politics at its worse has been: a highly combustible mixture that can, when ignited, maim or destroy those in its proximity.

If the trajectory of American history—or, at least, the present circumstances of the United States—yielded a serious possibility that in the years ahead religious faith will play a destructive role in American politics, it would make sense for us to reject Senator Lieberman's "case for allowing faith into politics" and to consider ways to marginalize the role of faith in politics. But the possibility that religion will play a destructive role is more remote than serious. The same survey data that shows that the United States is an increasingly religiously diverse society—perhaps the most religiously diverse society in the world—also shows that today most citizens of the United States are much more tolerant of their religious differences than were previous generations of Americans, and that they consider the religious diversity of the United States not as a problem to be endured or overcome but as a source of the nation's strength.[6] These are not the attitudes that fueled the religious wars of the sixteenth century; as John Courtney Murray admonished, we shouldn't "project into the future of the Republic the nightmares . . . of the past."[7] . . . A rapprochement between religion and politics forged in the crucible of a time or place very different from our own is not necessarily—not even probably—the best arrangement for our time and place. If in the years ahead the predominant mode of religious participation in politics is more ecumenical than sectarian, as befits a society as religiously diverse as the United States, the chance is slim to nonexistent that the mixture—religion and politics—will unite.[8]

Endnotes

[1] Christopher J. Eberle, *Religious Conviction in Liberal Politics.* (New York: Cambridge University Press, 2002).

[2] Diana Eck, *A New Religious America: How a "Christian Country" Has Become the World's Most Religiously Diverse Nation.* (San Francisco: Harper San Francisco, 2001).

[3] Sheler, "Faith in America" at 42.

[4] Joseph Cardinal Bernardin, "The Consistent Ethic of Life After Webster," 19 Origins 741, 748 (1990). See David Lockhead, *The Dialogical Imperative: A Christian Reflection on Innerfaith Encounter* (Maryknoll, NY: Orbis Books, 1988), at 93.

[5] Max Horkheimer and Theodor Adorno, quoted in Hans Küng, *Does God Exist?* (Garden City, NY: Double day, 1978), 490.

[6] Sheler, "Faith in America," see also Alan Wolfe, "Civil Religion Revisited: Quiet Faith in Middle Class America," in Nancy L. Rosenblum, ed., *Obligations of Citizenship and Demands of Faith: Religious Accommodations in Pluralist Democracies.* (Princeton, NJ: Princeton University Press, 2000), 32.

[7] John Courtney Murray, *We Hold these Truths* (Kansas City, MO: Sheed and Ward, 1960), 23–24.

[8] For discussion of the point, see Eberle, *Religious Conviction in Liberal Politics*, 152–186.

Religion, Democracy, and the "Twin Tolerations"

Alfred Stepan

Western Europe and the Twin Tolerations

How should one read the "lessons" of the historical relationship between Western Christianity and democracy? Here I would like to call particular attention to four possible misinterpretations. *Empirically,* we should beware of simple assertions about the actual existence of "separation of church and state" or the necessity of "secularism." *Doctrinally,* we should beware of assuming that any of the world's religious systems are univocally democratic or nondemocratic. *Methodologically,* we should beware of what I will call the "fallacy of unique founding conditions." And, *normatively,* we should beware of the liberal injunction, famously argued by the most influential contemporary political philosopher in the English language, John Rawls to "take the truths of religion off the political agenda."

 . . . What do contemporary West European constitutions and normal political practice indicate about the role of religious parties in government? Despite what Western analysts may think about the impropriety of religious-based parties ruling in a secular democracy like Turkey, Christian Democratic parties have frequently ruled in Germany, Austria, Italy, Belgium, and the Netherlands. The *only* EU member state whose constitution prohibits political parties from using religious affiliations or symbols is Portugal. Yet I should make two observations about this apparent anomaly. First, the article prohibiting the use of religious symbols by political parties in Portugal is a nondemocratic holdover from the constitution drafted in 1976 by a Constituent Assembly under heavy pressure from the revolutionary Armed Forces Movement and later revised (in 1982) to the Centro Democratico Social, which operates with full political freedom and is a member in good standing of all the International Christian Democratic organizations.

From: Stepan, Alfred. "Religion, Democracy, and the 'Twin Tolerations.'" *Journal of Democracy* 11:4 (2000), pp. 37–57. © National Endowment for Democracy and The Johns Hopkins University Press. Reprinted with permission of The Johns Hopkins University Press.

In the twentieth century, probably the two most "hostile" separations of church and state in Western Europe occurred in 1931 in Spain and in 1905 in France. Both of these countries, however, now have a "friendly" separation of church and state. In fact, since 1958, the French government has paid a substantial part of the cost of the Catholic Church's elementary school system. Virtually no Western European democracy now has a rigid or hostile separation of church and state. Most have arrived at a democratically negotiated freedom of religion from state interference, and all of them allow religious groups freedom not only to worship privately but to organize groups in civil society and political society. The "lesson" from Western Europe, therefore, lies *not* in the need for a "wall of separation" between church and state but in the constant political construction and reconstruction of the "twin tolerations." Indeed, it is only in the context of the "twin tolerations" that the concept of "separation of church and state" has a place in the modern vocabulary of West European democracy.

Unfinished Business

All the world's major religions today are involved in struggles over the twin tolerations. For Hinduism in India and Judaism in Israel, religion-state conflicts are now especially politically salient. In the first two decades of their independence after World War II, India and Israel were under the political and ideological hegemony of secular political leaders and parties. By the 1990s, however, both these secular political traditions were challenged by opposition movements that drew some of their support from forces seeking to redraw the boundaries of the "twin tolerations" to accommodate more fundamentalist and less tolerant visions of the polity.

In Israel, the state was originally a nationalist state for the Jewish people, but there are growing demands for it to be a religious state as well. There are also demands to make citizenship for the Arab minority less inclusive, and even to amend the Law of Return so as to give Orthodox rabbis the authority to determine whom the state of Israel recognizes as a Jew.

In India, after the 1998 and 1999 general elections, the Hindu revivalist BJP formed the government, in alliance with regional parties. Although it also contains more moderate elements, the BJP is pressured by its associated shock troops in uncivil society, such as the neofascist RSS, who want eventually to utilize the majority status of

Hindus to make India a state that would privilege Hindu values as they interpret them.

A major force opposing the BJP and the RSS is the Gandhian-Nehruvian strand of Hinduism, which insists that both India and Hinduism are multivocal and that the deepest values of Hinduism must respect the idea of India as a diverse, tolerant state rather than a nation-state of Hindus. Gandhi and Nehru knew that since India was a multicultural, multireligious, and multicommunity state, "nation-state building" would make it harder, not easier, to build democracy.

India is 17 times poorer than any OECD democracy. The support for democracy in India under such difficult conditions cannot be understood without an appreciation of the tremendous strength that Gandhi drew from some traditional Hindu religious values and styles of action in his peaceful struggles for independence, democracy, an end to "untouchability," and respect for Muslims.

If India, with 600 million non-Hindi speakers, 14 languages that are spoken by at least 10 million people, and a minority population of about 120 million Muslims, is to remain a democracy the voices of those who wish to make India a Hindu and Hindi nation-state must be countered by an ever stronger Gandhian voice speaking for India as a multireligious home to a billion people.

A more complete study of the themes raised in this brief essay would not only discuss religions I have omitted, but would analyze in much greater detail the emergence of the twin tolerations in the West. The establishment of state-sponsored churches in Scandinavia and Britain, while initially a way of securing political control of the church, eventually led not only to the "twin tolerations," but also, in the long run, to the "sociologically spontaneous secularization" of most of the population. Why?

Liberal scholars might also want to reconsider how liberal the anticlerical movements in France and Spain really were. What was the political effect of this liberalism from above? In Spain in the early 1930s, did liberal and socialist anticlericalism justify the tearing down of walls separating civil cemeteries from Jewish cemeteries? If the 1905 French liberal model of expropriating Jesuit property had been followed in the United States, Georgetown and many other Jesuit universities would have been expropriated. Would this have contributed to the strengthening of liberalism in the United States?

Another important area for further research is the role of the state in generating religious toleration. Scholars, especially sociologists of religion, have focused their attention on society-led movements toward tolerance, but at some critical moments state-led policies, such as those structured by Emperor Ferdinand I at the Peace of Augsburg of 1555, were crucial for ending society-led religious conflicts. Likewise, it was the Ottoman state that crafted the millets, with their extraordinary tolerance for religious self-government by minority national religious communities. There are many more examples of state-led tolerance, as well as state-led intolerance, that we need to study.

Finally, even the separation of church and state originally mandated by the U.S. Constitution's First Amendment ("Congress shall make no law respecting an establishment of religion, or prohibiting the free exercise thereof") is misunderstood today by many U.S. citizens. The amendment did not prohibit the 13 original states from having *their own established religions*. It merely prohibited the Congress from establishing one official religion for the United States *as a whole*. In fact, on the eve of the revolution, only three of the 13 colonies—Rhode Island, Pennsylvania, and Delaware—had no provision for an established church. Even after the revolution, the South Carolina constitution of 1778 established the "Christian Protestant Religion." Four New England states continued for some time to maintain state-subsidized, largely Congregational, churches. The eventual political construction of the West's strongest wall separating church and state along with the social emergence of one of the West's most churchgoing, and most fundamentalist populations, is yet another "crooked path" of toleration and intoleration that needs further study and reflection.

Discussion questions for II - A

1. More and more, there is talk in the media of an all out war–or clash of civilizations between the West and Muslim fundamentalism. Peter Berger sees the situation with far more nuance. How do you assess the situation?
2. George Weigel cites examples of Catholicism playing a major role in overthrowing dictatorial communist regimes at the end of the 20th century. What do you think about these examples with regard to the church's championing of human rights and social justice?
3. Abdullahi A. An-Na'im illuminates the distinctions between Western and Islamic thought on secularism, and guards against equating a moderate Muslim position with that of a fundamentalist view. Can you discuss the difference?
4. Vaclav Havel argues against a purely secular view of democracy– yet his definition of the divine is very broad and unrestrictive. How does the idea work for a secularist? For a more conventional religionist?
5. Charles Kimball cites ten key practices as part of a "just peacemaking paradigm" developed by some Christian ethicists in recent times. Comment on their worth and the prospects for their adoption.
6. Why is Michael Perry optimistic about the role that religion will play in the future in strengthening American democracy?
7. Alfred Stepan discusses the need for "twin tolerations" and not separation of church and state. What does he mean by that? Do you believe that it is a more effective approach to the peaceful and productive coexistence of church and state?

II - B

Encounters Marked by
Nuance and Complexity

Relationships between religion and democracy have been various through history, ranging from accommodating to warring. The "sacred" wall between church and state in the United States is only one approach to the protection of both church and state. Other democratic nations have chosen a variety of other paths. But all these relationships, perhaps for better *and* worse, are complex and nuanced. Centuries ago, we learn from Amartya Sen, Indians brought to China the Buddhist tradition that did as much or more to democratize Chinese society as it did to enhance the spiritual life of the Chinese people. In modern times, we see that religious leaders on both ends of the left-right spectrum are helping their followers to find common ground. These signs that we find in history and in our own time can be heartening for those who have feared that fundamentalism would be the guiding religious and political principle of the 21st century.

An Islamic Democracy for Iraq?

Ian Buruma

Is "Islamic Democracy" really possible? Or is it something meaning-less, like "Jewish science," say or contradictory, like "people's demo-cracy" under Communism? This is the question that will determine the future of Iraq, since the man with the greatest credibility in that broken country is Grand Ayatollah Ali al-Sistani, the Shiite cleric, who refuses to run for office himself but says that he supports the idea of Islamic Democracy.

Islamic Democracy has no track record, since it barely exists as yet. In Iran, a democracy of sorts is controlled by a religious council. Perhaps Turkey comes closest to a European model we know, based loosely on religious values without being a theocracy. Yet even Turkish democracy is distrusted by many Europeans and is actually considered sinful by some Muslims.

The idea that modern democracy has to be secular in its ethos is, of course, rooted in European history. The Enlightenment was partly an assault on the authority of the church, especially in France. Political arrangements were to be subject to reason, not to theology. To be mod-ern was to reject religion, or "superstition," and to believe in science. It was not enough in the view of Voltaire, among others, to put organ-ized religion in its place; it was necessary to "wipe out that rubbish." The belief in science as a solution for all human problems became a kind of superstition itself. Scientific socialism, à la Stalin and Mao, for example, led to all manner of crackpot experiments that caused the deaths of millions.

Of course, not all rationalists were so extreme. Many typical Enlightenment thinkers, like John Locke, were convinced that a political system based on enlightened self-interest could not survive without a strong basis in religious morality. The kind of anti-clericalism that inspired Stalinists and other authoritarians was more a product of the French Revolution than of the pursuit of democracy in itself.

From "An Islamic Democracy for Iraq?" First published in *The New York Times Magazine* © 2005. Reprinted with permission of the Wylie Agency.

In fact, anti-clericalism, much more than a history of religious zeal, formed the basis for many of the Middle East's bloodiest political failures: Nasserism in Egypt, Baathism in Syria and Iraq, the Shah in Iran. These regimes were led by secular elites who saw religion as something that held their countries back or in a state of colonial dependence. The fact is that a number of iron-fisted reformers, objects of assassination attempts by religious zealots, showed the gap between the secular "progressive" elites and the people they ruled. When organized religion is destroyed, something worse often takes its place, usually a quasi religion or personality cult exploited by dictators. When it is marginalized, as happened in Egypt and other part of the Middle East, it provokes a religious rebellion. This is not to say that Muslim clerics are naturally disposed to democracy. But, as Michael Hirsh pointed out in a recent article in The Washington Monthly, a number of Middle East scholars—Richard Bulliet, author of "The Case for Islamo-Christian Civilization," among them—have argued that religion for many centuries actually acted as a constraint on tyranny in the Muslim world. The destruction of traditional Muslim institutions, like religious schools and mosques, in the name of modernization left a social void in which extreme, political Islam would eventually thrive.

Ayatollah Khomeini was not acting as a traditional Shiite cleric but as a modern revolutionary who took power as a political strongman. And in the eyes of many believers, his worldly dictatorship in Iran undermined his stature as a religious figure, since mullahs are not supposed to act like politicians. Osama bin Laden is an amateur priest with more knowledge of Swiss bank transfers and media manipulation than of the intricacies of Islam. It would be hard to find a serious Muslim cleric or scholar who respects him.

It may be useful to reflect for a moment on how the West itself has coped with religion. The separation of church and state was indeed a necessary condition for democratic development in Europe and the United States, but the separation has never been absolute. Britain's constitutional arrangements include organized religion: the monarch is the protector of the Anglican faith. This may now be nothing more than a formality, but in continental European politics Christian democratic parties are still the mainstream. The first such party, the Anti-Revolutionary Party, was founded in 1879 by a Calvinist ex-pastor in the Netherlands named Abraham Kuyper. His aim was to restore God (not the church) as the absolute sovereign over human affairs. Only if secular government was firmly embedded in the Christian faith could its democratic institutions survive. That is what he believed and what Christian Democrats still believe.

I do not believe this. It is always tricky for an agnostic in religious affairs to argue for the importance of organized religion, but I would argue not that more people should be religious or that democracy cannot survive without God, but that the voices of religious people should be heard. The most important condition for a functional democracy is that people take part. If religious affiliations provide the necessary consensus to play by common rules, then they should be recognized. A Sharia-based Shiite theocracy, even if it were supported by a majority, would not be a democracy. Only if the rights and interests of the various ethnic and religious groups are negotiated and compromises reached could you speak of a functioning democracy.

A tall order, to be sure, but given the miserable record of secular politics in the Middle East, and beyond, it makes sense that several distinguished experts on Islam have taken issue with the Ataturkian solution in Iraq. Reuel Marc Gerecht, a fellow of the American Enterprise Institute for Public Policy Research and a former CIA specialist, has argued that devout followers of Sistani offer not just the best hope for democracy but also the only one. In Gerecht's view, Sistani's "Iranian blood and family in the Islamic republic has surely made [him] more sensitive to the pitfalls of clerical dictatorship," and "in the matter of democracy in Iraq, Sistani may again become one of American's most effective allies." Noah Feldman, an NYU law professor, has also argued forcefully that Islamic democracy is possible in Iraq, a democracy that guarantees not just that people can vote but also that they can "vote for laws infused with Islamic beliefs, ideals and values, and the state can endorse Islam, and fund religious institutions and education."

Will Iraq be like Indonesia? Will democracy allow the differences between Arabs and Kurds, Shiites and Sunnis, religious and secular, to be solved without violence? In principle, you would have to say that it would. But the Iraqis have problems that the Indonesians did not have to face. They have to build democratic institutions under a hated foreign occupation.

It is very difficult to build a democracy as pupils of foreign tutors who arrived in bombers and tanks. Even though the foreign occupiers say they want an Iraqi democracy too, anyone or any party believed to be on the side of foreigners is discredited from the start. The more those foreigners insist on secularism, the more the local people may turn to radical Islamism. And the more violence the Islamists unleash, the less likely it is that Iraqis can vote in safety. This is particularly true of the so-called Sunni triangle north and west of Baghdad. It is all very well for Secretary of Defense Donald Rumsfeld, and for leading Shiites and Kurds, to say that it would still be better to have elections, even if many people can't take part, but that won't do. "There is no perfect election in the world," Sa-ad Jawad Qandil told *The Boston Globe*. Qandil is a senior official in the Supreme Council for the Islamic Revolution, a major Shiite party better known as Sciri. "If there are some minorities who cannot participate because of security, that is not reason to cancel the decision of the majority." Well, yes, it is. For if the Sunnis can't vote, Iraqi democracy won't work, because without the consent of this minority, the majority can never govern in peace.

There are other problems with a democracy incorporating a patchwork of faiths and denominations. Without a two-party system, small parties can have too much influence, as they do in Israel. Most Israelis are secular people, but tiny orthodox parties can sometimes make or break governments. Perhaps the early Zionists, almost all secular, socialist kibbutzniks, gave too much away to the religious, by letting them set the rules for marriage, among other things. The fear was that without such a deal, the ultra-Orthodox would not recognize the state of Israel. But the founding fathers of Israel cannot have anticipated that autonomy in spiritual affairs would lead to so much clout in secular politics.

It is also true that the religious, in Europe, the United States or anywhere, often do what their priests or mullahs tell them to. Until not so long ago, many people in countries with Catholic or Protestant parties did just that. But at least they voted, and by consenting to the democratic rules, they managed to live together without going at one another's throats. If Shiites and Sunnis can do so in a future Iraq, by voting for religious parties, then so be it. But first they have to be able to vote without getting killed. That is the issue, and not religion per se. The answer will be shaped by a foreign occupation, which made democracy possible, but then, by its very presence, might help to snuff it out.

Passage to China

Amartya Sen

The intellectual links between China and India, stretching over two thousand years, have had far-reaching effects on the history of both countries, yet they are hardly remembered today. What little notice they get tends to come from writers interested in religious history, particularly the history of Buddhism, which began its spread from India to China in the first century. In China, Buddhism became a powerful force until it was largely displaced by Confucianism and Taoism approximately a thousand years later. But religion is only one part of the much bigger story of Sino-Indian connections during the first millennium. A broader understanding of these relations is greatly needed, not only for us to appreciate more fully the history of a third of the world's population, but also because the connections between the two countries are important for political and social issues today.

Certainly religion has been a major source of contact between China and India, and Buddhism was central to the movement of people and ideas between the two countries. But the wider influence of Buddhism was not confined to religion. Its secular impact stretched into science, mathematics, literature, linguistics, architecture, medicine, and music. We know from the elaborate accounts left by a number of Chinese visitors to India, such as Faxian in the fifth century and Xuanzang and Yi Jing in the seventh, that their interest was by no means restricted to religious theory and practices. Similarly, the Indian scholars who went to China, especially in the seventh and eighth centuries, included not only religious experts but also other professionals such as astronomers and mathematicians. In the eighth century an Indian astronomer named Gautama Siddhartha became the president of the Board of Astronomy in China.

The richness and variety of early intellectual relations between China and India have long been obscured. This neglect is now

This is an excerpt from Amartya Sen's "Passage to China," *The New York Review of Books*, Dec 2, 2004 and the reader is encouraged to look at the full text since only a small part of the essay has been reproduced here.

reinforced by the contemporary tendency to classify the world's population into distinct "civilizations" defined largely by religion (for example Samuel Huntington's partitioning of the world into such categories as "Western civilization," "Islamic civilization," and "Hindu civilization"). There is, as a result, a widespread inclination to understand people mainly through their religious beliefs, even if this misses much that is important about them. The limitations of this perspective have already done significant harm to our understanding of other aspects of the global history of ideas. Many are now predisposed to see the history of Muslims as quintessentially Islamic history, ignoring the flowering of science, mathematics, and literature that was made possible by Muslim intellectuals, particularly between the eighth and the thirteenth centuries. One result of such a narrow emphasis on religion is that a disaffected Arab activist today is encouraged to take pride only in the purity of Islam, rather than in the diversity and richness of Arab history. In India too, there are frequent attempts to portray the broad civilization of India as "Hindu civilization"—to use the phrase favored both by theorists like Samuel Huntington and by Hindu political activists.

Second, there is an odd and distracting contrast between the ways in which Western and non-Western ideas and scholarship are currently understood. In interpreting non-Western works, many commentators tend to ascribe a much greater importance to religion than is merited, neglecting the works' secular interests. Few assume that, say, Isaac Newton's scientific work must be understood as primarily Christian (even though he did have Christian beliefs); nor do most of us take it for granted that his contributions to scientific knowledge must somehow be interpreted in the light of his deep interest in mysticism (important as mystical speculations were to him, perhaps even motivating some of his scientific work). In contrast, when it comes to non-Western cultures, religious reductionism tends to be a powerful influence. Scholars often presume that none of the broadly conceived intellectual work of Buddhist scholars, or of followers of Tantric practices, could be "properly understood" except in the special light of their religious beliefs and customs.

The transfer of ideas and skills in mathematics and science remains central to the contemporary commercial world whether for the development of information technology or of modern industrial methods. What may perhaps be less clear is how nations learn from one another both in enlarging the scope of public communication and in improving public health care. As it happens, both were important in the intellectual relations between China and India in the first millennium and remain central even today.

As a religion, Buddhism began with at least two specific characteristics that were quite unusual, its agnosticism and its commitment to broad discussion of public issues. Some of the earliest open public meetings on record, aimed specifically at settling disputes over religious beliefs as well as other matters, took place in India in elaborately organized Buddhist "councils," in which adherents of different points of view argued their differences. The first of these large councils was held in Rajagriha shortly after Gautama Buddha's death 2,500 years ago. The largest of the councils, the third, was held in the capital city of Patna, under the patronage of emperor Ashoka in the third century BCE. Ashoka also tried to codify and circulate what must have been among the earliest formulations of rules for public discussion—a kind of ancient version of *Robert's Rules of Order*. He demanded, for example, "restraint in regard to speech, so that there should be no extolling of one's own sect or disparaging of other sects on inappropriate occasions, and it should be moderate even in appropriate occasions." Even when engaged in arguing, "other sects should be duly honored in every way on all occasions."

Insofar as reasoned public discussion is central to democracy (as John Stuart Mill, John Rawls, and Jurgen Habermas, among many others, have argued), the origins of democracy can indeed be traced in part to the tradition of public discussion that received much encouragement from the emphasis on dialogue in Buddhism in both India and China (and also in Japan, Korea, and elsewhere). It is also significant that nearly every attempt at early printing in China, Korea, and Japan was undertaken by Buddhists.[1] The first printed book in the world (or rather, the first printed book that is actually dated) was the Chinese translation of an Indian Sanskrit treatise, the so-called *Diamond Sutra*, which was printed in China in 868 AD. While the *Diamond Sutra* is almost entirely a religious document, the boldly inscribed dedication of this ninth-century book, "for universal free distribution," announces a commitment to public education.

John Kieschnick has noted that "one of the reasons for the important place of books in the Chinese Buddhist tradition is the belief that one can gain merit by copying or printing Buddhist scriptures," and he has argued that "the origins of this belief can be traced to India."[2] There is some ground for that view; there is also surely a connection here with the emphasis on communication with a broad public by such Buddhist leaders as Ashoka, who erected throughout India large stone tablets bearing inscriptions describing the qualities of good public behavior (including the rules on how to conduct an argument).

The development of printing, of course, had a powerful effect on the development of democracy, but even in the short run, it opened new possibilities for public communication and had enormous consequences for social and political life in China. Among other things, it also influenced neo-Confucian education, and as Theodore de Bary has noted, "women's education achieved a new level of importance with the rise of . . . learning [during the Song dynasty] and its neo-Confucian extensions in the Ming, marked by the great spread of printing, literacy, and schooling."[3]

Endnotes

[1] Needham, *Science and Civilization in China*, Vol. 5, Part 1, pp. 148–149.

[2] Kieschnick, *The Impact of Buddhism on Chinese Material Culture*, p. 164.

[3] Wm. Theodore de Bary, "Neo-Confucian Education," in *Sources of Chinese Tradition*, compiled by W. Theodore de Bary and Irene Bloom (Columbia University Press, second edition, 1999), Vol. 1., p. 820.

More Religion, but Not the Old-Time Kind

Laurie Goodstein

Almost anywhere you look around the world, with the glaring exception of Western Europe, religion is now a rising force. Former Communist countries are humming with mosque builders, Christian missionaries and freelance spiritual entrepreneurs of every possible persuasion. In China, underground "house churches" are proliferating so quickly that neither the authorities nor Christian leaders can keep reliable count. In much of South and Central America, exuberant Pentecostal churches, where worshipers catch the Holy Spirit and speak in tongues, continue to spread, challenging the Roman Catholic tradition. And in the United States, religious conservatives, triumphant over their role in the re-election of President Bush, are increasingly asserting their power in politics, the media and culture.

The tsunami in Asia could spur religious revival as well, as victims and onlookers turn to mosques, temples and churches both to help them fathom the catastrophe and to provide humanitarian assistance.

What does all this rising religiosity add up to? It is easy to assume that a more religious world means a more fractious world, where violent conflict is fueled by violent fundamentalist movements. But some religion experts say that while it is clear that religiosity is on the rise, it is not at all clear that fundamentalism is. Indeed, there may be a rising backlash against violent fundamentalism of any faith.

The world's fastest growing religion is not any type of fundamentalism, but the Pentecostal wing of Christianity. While Christian fundamentalists are focused on doctrine and the inerrancy of Scripture, what is most important for Pentecostals is what they call "spirit-filled" worship, including speaking in tongues and miracle healing. Brazil, where American missionaries planted Pentecostalism in the early 20th century, now has a congregation with its own TV station, soccer team and political party.

Most scholars of Christianity believe that the world's largest church is a Pentecostal one—the Yoido Full Gospel Church in Seoul, South

Korea, which was founded in 1958 by a converted Buddhist who held a prayer meeting in a tent he set up in a slum. More than 250,000 people show up for worship on a typical Sunday. "If I were to buy stock in global Christianity, I would buy it in Pentecostalism," said Martin E. Marty, professor emeritus of the history of Christianity at the University of Chicago Divinity School and a coauthor of a study of fundamentalist movements. "I would not buy it in fundamentalism."

After the American presidential election in November, some liberal commentators warned that the nation was on the verge of a takeover by Christian "fundamentalists." But in the United States today, most of the Protestants who make up what some call the Christian right are not fundamentalists, who are more prone to create separatist enclaves, but evangelicals, who engage the culture and share their faith. Professor Marty defines fundamentalism as essentially a backlash against secularism and modernity.

For example, at the fundamentalist Bob Jones University, in Greenville, S.C., students are not allowed to listen to contemporary music of any kind, even Christian rock or rap. But at Wheaton College in Illinois, a leading evangelical school, contemporary Christian music is regular fare for many students.

Christian fundamentalism emerged in the United States in the 1920's, but was already in decline by the 1960's. By then, it had been superceded by evangelicalism, with its Billy Graham-style revival meetings, radio stations and seminaries. The word "fundamentalist" itself has fallen out of favor among conservative Christians in the United States, not least because it has come to be associated with extremism and violence overseas.

Fundamentalism in non-Christian faiths became a phenomenon in the rest of the world in the 1970's with "the failure and the bankruptcy of secular, nationalistic liberal creeds around the world," said Philip Jenkins, a professor of history and religious studies at Pennsylvania State University. Among the "creeds cracking up" were nationalism, Marxism, socialism, pan-Arabism and pan-Africanism. "From the 1970's on, you get the growth of not just more conservative religion, but religion with a political bent," said Professor Jenkins, the author of "The Next Christendom: The Coming of Global Christianity."

Now, the future of fundamentalism is murky, with several contradictory trends at work simultaneously. There is little doubt that one fundamentalism can feed another, spurring recruitment and escalating into a sort of religious arms race. In Nigeria's central Plateau State,

Muslim and Christian gangs have razed one another's villages in the last few years, leaving tens of thousands of dead and displaced. In rioting in India in 2002, more than 1,000 people, most of them Muslims, were killed by Hindus in Gujarat state—retaliation for a Muslim attack a day earlier on a train full of Hindus, which killed 59.

Husain Haqqani, a Pakistani political commentator and visiting scholar at the Carnegie Endowment for International Peace in Washington, said that insurgents in Falluja, Iraq, recruited fighters with the false rumor that Christian crusaders with the Rev. Franklin Graham's aid organization, Samaritan's Purse, were on the way over to convert Muslims. (Mr. Graham is known throughout the Muslim world for his statement that Islam is a "very evil and wicked religion.") Fundamentalism does not necessarily lead to intolerance, said Professor Jenkins of Pennsylvania State. "People with very convinced, traditional views can get along together for a very long time," he said. "But sometimes we get into cycles where they can't, and we seem to be in one of those cycles right now."

Analysts are also seeing signs of a backlash as religious believers grow disenchanted with movements that have produced little but bloodshed, economic stagnation and social repression. In last year's elections in India, voters repudiated the ruling Bharatiya Janata Party, a Hindu nationalist group whose cadres had helped stir up violence in some Indian states against Muslims and others.

And in Indonesia, the world's largest Muslim country, mainstream Islamic groups in September helped elect as president a secular general who had been relatively outspoken about the threat posed by the radical group Jemaah Islamiyah, which is responsible for several acts of terrorism, including the bombing in Bali in 2002.

Fundamentalist movements also stumble because they plan for the overthrow, but not for the governing. Half the Muslim world is illiterate, Mr. Haqqani said, but the Taliban didn't make a dent in improving literacy when it ruled in Afghanistan. If Iran had a free and fair plebiscite today, Professor Marty said, "the ayatollahs would be dumped."

For reasons like this, said R. Scott Appleby, a history professor at the University of Notre Dame and director of the Joan B. Kroc Institute for International Peace Studies, "it would be misleading to say fundamentalism is on the rise now." He added: "I would say we're just more aware of it because these people are better organized, more mobile and more vocal than ever before."

In 2003, Professor Appleby and two other scholars, Gabriel A. Almond and Emmanuel Sivan, published "Strong Religion," a book based on research done with Professor Marty for the Fundamentalism Project. The book's subtitle was the "The Rise of Fundamentalisms Around the World." Now, Mr. Appleby said, "There is some evidence, some literature that says fundamentalism is on the decline, that it has peaked or is peaking precisely because it has a tendency toward violence and intolerance, and those ultimately don't work. . . . They lead to bloodshed, loss of life, and no recognizable economic upturn, and there is an exhaustion with it."

Church Meets State

Mark Lilla

Everyone, it seems, wants to get religion. Since the re-election of George W. Bush our magazines and newspapers have been playing catch-up, running long articles on the evangelicals and fundamentalists, an alien world the press typically ignores. Anxious Democratic strategists have issued pleas to find common ground with the religious center on issues like abortion, and elected officials have dutifully begun baring their souls in public. This is a media bubble, and like all bubbles it will burst. Far more interesting and consequential has been the effort to reinterpret history to give religion a more central place in America's past—and, perhaps, in its future.

At the low end there is the schlock history written by religious propagandists like David Barton, the author of the bizarre pastiche "The Myth of Separation," who use selective quotations out of context to suggest that the framers were inspired believers who thought they were founding a Christian nation. But there is also serious work being done by historians like Mark Noll and George Marsden to counter the tendency in American historiography to rummage through the past for anticipations of our secular, egalitarian, multicultural present. This is a useful corrective and reminds us that the role of religion in American life was large and the separation of church and state less clear than today.

At the highest end there has been a new scholarly look at the history of the modern political ideas that eventually put America on its special path. The best example is Gertrude Himmelfarb's important study, "The Roads to Modernity." Here the argument is that, unlike the anticlerical *philosophes* of the French Enlightenment, the British and American thinkers of the 18th century looked favorably on religion as a support to modern democracy. They saw that it could assist in forming good citizens by providing moral education and helping people be self-reliant. By teaching people to work, save and give, religion could prove a ballast to the self-destructive tendencies of both capitalism and democracy. There is, therefore, nothing antimodern or even antiliberal in encouraging American religion and making room for it in public life.

As intellectual history, this is a sound thesis. It is, however, incomplete, which is why we should be wary of drawing contemporary lessons from it. In truth, the leaders of the British and American Enlightenments shared the same hope as the French *lumières*: that the centuries-old struggle between church and state could be brought to an end, and along with it the fanaticism, superstition and obscurantism into which Christian culture had sunk. What distinguished thinkers like David Hume and John Adams from their French counterparts was not their ultimate aims; it was their understanding of religious psychology. The British and Americans made two wagers. The first was that religious sects, if they were guaranteed liberty, would grow attached to liberal democracy and obey its norms. The second was that entering the public square would liberalize them doctrinally, that they would become less credulous and dogmatic, more sober and rational.

The first wager is well known, the second less so—though it is probably the more important one. In fact, it is difficult to imagine the relative peace of American church-state relations without the liberalization of Protestant theology in the 19th century. "Liberal" in the theological sense means several things. It includes a critical approach to Scripture as a historical document, an openness to modern science, a turn from public ritual to private belief and a search for common ground in the Bible's moral message. Theological liberalism drew from many sources—the English deists, Rousseau's romanticism, the philosophical idealism of Kant and Hegel. And thanks to Friedrich Schleiermacher and his 19th-century disciples it became the dominant school of Protestant theology, first in Germany, then in Britain and the United States. To many it appeared to fulfill the hope of a modern, reformed Christianity helping to shape citizens in modern, liberal-democratic polities.

But theological liberalism collapsed suddenly and dramatically in early 20th-century Germany, for reasons Americans would do well to ponder. The crisis was essentially spiritual but had wide political reverberations. Thinkers and ordinary believers began yearning for a more dynamic and critical faith, one that would stand in judgment over the modern world, not lend it support. They sought an authentic experience with the divine, genuine spiritual solace and a clear understanding of the one path to salvation. And what did liberal Protestantism teach? In the words of H. Richard Niebuhr, that "a God without wrath brought men without sin into a kingdom without judgment through the ministrations of a Christ without a cross." And if that was the case, why be a Christian at all?

The carnage of World War I seemed to answer that question. The lesson drawn was that Christianity had been seduced by bourgeois, democratic society when it should have been bringing God's judgment down upon it. The liberal movement fell apart during the Weimar period, and from its ashes sprouted a wild array of religious tendencies, some ecstatic and mystical, some politically driven. Those who were politically engaged could be found all over the map, from the socialist left to the fascist right—everywhere, it seemed, but in the liberal-democratic center.

If this story sounds somewhat familiar, it should. After the last Great Awakening at the end of the 19th century, liberal theology made steady gains in all the mainline American churches, and by the 1950's it represented the consensus within Protestantism, and was also softening the edges of American Catholicism and Judaism. Yet it, too, has now collapsed. Over the past 30 years we have seen the steady decline of mainline faiths and the upsurge of evangelical, Pentecostal, charismatic and "neo-orthodox" movements—not only among Protestants but among Catholics and Jews as well. Politics played a large role in this, especially divisions over the Vietnam War and the cultural transformations since the 1960's. But the deepest dynamics were again spiritual.

It appears that there are limits to the liberalization of biblical religion. The more the Bible is treated as a historical document, the more its message is interpreted in universalist terms, the more the churches sanctify the political and cultural order, the less hold liberal religion will eventually have on the hearts and minds of believers. This dynamic is particularly pronounced in Protestantism, which heightens the theological tension brought on by being in the world but not of it. Liberal religion imagines a pacified order in which good citizenship, good morals and rational belief coexist harmoniously. It is therefore unprepared when the messianic and eschatological forces of biblical faith begin to stir.

The leading thinkers of the British and American Enlightenments hoped that life in a modern democratic order would shift the focus of Christianity from a faith-based reality to a reality-based faith. American religion is moving in the opposite direction today, back toward the ecstatic, literalist and credulous spirit of the Great Awakenings. Its most disturbing manifestations are not political, at least not yet. They are cultural. The fascination with the "end times," the belief in personal (and self-serving) miracles, the ignorance of basic science and history, the demonization of popular culture, the censoring of textbooks, the separatist instincts of the home-schooling movement—all these developments are far more worrying in the long term than the loss of a few Congressional seats.

No one can know how long this dumbing-down of American religion will persist. But so long as it does, citizens should probably be more vigilant about policing the public square, not less so. If there is anything David Hume and John Adams understood, it is that you cannot sustain liberal democracy without cultivating liberal habits of mind among religious believers. That remains true today, both in Baghdad and in Baton Rouge.

Religious Right, Left Meet in Middle
Clergy Aim to Show That Faith Unifies

Alan Cooperman

The Rev. Rob Schenck is an evangelical Christian and a leader of the religious right. Rabbi David Saperstein is a Reform Jew and a leader of the religious left. Both head political advocacy groups in Washington, and they have battled for years over abortion, gay rights, stem cell research and school prayer.

This summer, each intends to preach a bit of the other's usual message.

Schenck said he plans to tell young evangelicals at a Christian music festival on July 1 that homosexuality is not a choice but a "predisposition," something "deeply rooted" in many people. "That may not sound shocking to you, but it will be shocking to my audience," he said.

Saperstein said he is circulating a paper urging political moderates and liberals to "demonstrate their commitment to reduce abortions" by starting a campaign to reduce the number by half within two years.

Schenck and Saperstein disclosed their plans in separate interviews. They are not working together. The minister remains a die-hard opponent of same-sex marriage; the rabbi staunchly supports a woman's constitutional right to choose an abortion. But both are trying to find common ground between liberals and conservatives on moral issues— and they are not alone.

After a year in which religion played a polarizing role in U.S. politics, many religious leaders are eager to demonstrate that faith can be a uniter, not just a divider. The buzzwords today in pulpits and seminaries are crossover, convergence, common cause and shared values.

Last week in Washington, representatives of more than 40 U.S. denominations took part in the Convocation on Hunger at the National Cathedral, where they sang a Tanzanian hymn while the choir director shook a gourd full of seeds and children laid breads from around the world on the altar.

It may have been mistaken for a hippie ceremony were it not for the sight of clergy from the Southern Baptist Convention, Assemblies of God and other evangelical churches praying alongside Muslims, Buddhists, Sikhs, Roman Catholics, Greek Orthodox, mainline Protestants and Jews.

The show of solidarity was partly a reaction against "the recent manipulation of religion in ways that are divisive and partisan," said David Beckmann, a Lutheran minister and president of Bread for the World, a nonprofit group that helped organize the service.

"Because religion has been dragged into political life in some ways, this is the religious leadership of the nation saying, 'No, let us show you what religion in the public square should really be about,' "he said.

Meanwhile, the United Methodist Church, Episcopal Church and Evangelical Lutheran Church in America are moving quickly toward full communion, which would allow them to swap clergy and recognize one another's sacraments. Protestant and Jewish leaders, who have been at loggerheads over proposals to divest stock in companies that help Israel maintain control of the Palestinian territories, have announced a joint trip to the Holy Land in September.

The National Association of Evangelicals is promoting dialogue with Muslims, to discuss concerns for the environment and efforts to combat poverty. "On issues like poverty, the cold war among religious groups is over," said the Rev. Richard Cizik, its vice president for public policy.

The Rev. Don Argue, a past president of the NAE, is an informal adviser to Sen. Hillary Rodham Clinton (D-N.Y.), who has introduced legislation aimed at reducing the demand for abortions without restricting their availability. Jim Wallis, a left-leaning evangelical whose bestselling book "God's Politics" is a plea for liberals and conservatives to identify common causes, has worked with the staff of Sen. Rick Santorum (R-Pa.), as well as with Democrats on antipoverty proposals.

Some observers view all this aisle-crossing mainly as political positioning.

"There's a kind of pulling back from religious war," said Mark R. Silk, director of the Center for the Study of Religion in Public Life at Trinity College in Hartford, Conn. "But I don't think one should overlook the self-interest of both sides, at this moment, in positioning themselves as willing to compromise and work with the other side."

In last year's presidential election, voters who said they attend church more than once a week favored President Bush over Sen. John F. Kerry (D-Mass.) by a ratio of nearly 2 to 1. White evangelicals backed Bush by almost 4 to 1. Occasional (less than weekly) church-goers tilted narrowly toward Kerry, and secular voters overwhelmingly favored the Democrat, according to exit polls.

Religion was not just a defining issue in the campaign but a divisive one. Some Catholics questioned Kerry's worthiness to receive Holy Communion because of his stand on abortion rights. Church-based activists pushed referendums on same-sex marriage onto 13 state ballots.

Since the election, Democrats on Capitol Hill have tried to demonstrate that their positions are infused by faith; Republicans have sought to show that their moral concerns go beyond abortion and same-sex marriage.

"On the left, they need to show they have a religious bone in their body. On the right, they have to prove their vaunted values are not limited to one or two hot-button issues," Silk said. "So count me a little skeptical about how far this 'crossover' and 'convergence' really goes."

Saperstein, who heads the Religious Action Center, the Washington advocacy arm of the Reform movement in Judaism, said he believes the search for common ground is "both strategic and substantive."

"I think it's genuine and real, this engagement of liberals in trying to cut the number of abortions in this country," he said. "And I think conservatives are sincere when they say, 'I may be against gay marriage, but the demonization of gays and lesbians is deeply troubling to me,' or when they say, 'You can't look at the Bible without seeing the call to care for the poor.'"

Saperstein noted that the phenomenon of strange bedfellows began a decade ago on foreign policy. During the Clinton administration, the rock star Bono, former senator Jesse Helms (R-N.C.) and religious leaders across the political spectrum teamed up to champion debt relief for Africa. Since Bush took office, broad religious coalitions have backed U.S. peacemaking efforts in Sudan, funding to combat AIDS and pressure on countries that restrict religious freedom.

What is new, the rabbi said, is the effort to forge such coalitions on domestic issues.

"For 25 years, evangelicals involved in conservative politics and mainline denominations involved in liberal politics really have been adversaries, both in politics and in the free market of ideas, and that continues because we have very different visions of religion in American public life, and very different views of the Constitution, and very different views on some core issues," he said.

"But right now on abortion, poverty, gay issues, the environment, there's a lot of talk about crossing the lines and finding common ground. There are elements of a common vision, but not yet common policy or legislative proposals."

Schenck, who is president of Faith and Action, an evangelical organization on Capitol Hill, said that a willingness to reach across partisan lines is attractive, particularly to young people. "I think evangelicals are awakening to the vulnerability to being used in a political way. I hear a lot of people talking about that, about not being owned by a political party," he said.

Schenck outlined his limits: "There is no room for compromise on the sanctity of human life, the sanctity of marriage and the public acknowledgement of God." But he said that when he preaches at the Creation Festival, a four-day Christian music event in Mount Union, PA, he will say that the Bible forbids homosexual acts but that evangelicals are wrong to insist that sexual orientation is a matter of choice.

"As far as affirming that there may be people in our midst who have this as their nature, that will be radical within evangelical circles, because we want to see this purely as an act of will, like breaking and entering," he said. "And it just isn't that. It is so much more complex. If young people hear Christian leaders like me say that, I think they'll be interested in hearing what more we have to say."

Reinvigorate America's True Values

Nadine Strossen

When he first ran for President, George W. Bush famously proclaimed that his favorite political philosopher was Jesus Christ. As president, he has called U.S. counterterrorism efforts a "crusade." And, while campaigning for reelection, Bush used so much biblical, evangelical rhetoric that one might have thought he was running for church deacon, not leader of a diverse, democratic, and ostensibly secular nation. In exit polls, those who cited "moral values" as the 2004 election's most important issue overwhelmingly backed Bush– 79% voting for him, in contrast to 18% for John Kerry.

No wonder the Christian Right is claiming credit for Bush's victory.

Deeply religious people running for or serving in office is certainly not inherently antithetical to either good government or civil liberties. Many of our nation's most effective leaders, including some who have made outstanding contributions to civil liberties, have been devout religious believers and even religious leaders. Prominent modern examples include Reverend Martin Luther King, Jr. and Supreme Court Justice William Brennan.

But President Bush has gone further. He has cited his religious beliefs in support of public policy positions that threaten civil liberties, including his "faith-based initiatives," which force taxpayers to fund social services programs that discriminate on the basis of religion. Moreover, the religious conservatives who take credit for Bush's reelection have made clear that they expect him to promote further measures that are consistent with their own religious values, but inconsistent with our nation's constitutional values. Here, for instance, is a portion of the congratulatory letter that Dr. Bob Jones III, president of Bob Jones University, sent to Bush, following his electoral victory:

"In your re-election, God has graciously granted America—though she doesn't deserve it—a reprieve from the agenda of paganism

Discussion Questions for II - B

1. Ian Buruma asks, in his article, "An Islamic Democracy for Iraq?" if it is possible for a nation to be Islamic and democratic at the same time. The key to the peaceful coexistence of religion and democracy, he claims, is that "the voices of religious people should be heard. The most important condition for a functional democracy is that people take part." Europeans and Americans have different ways of accommodating the coexistence of democracy and religion. While Americans are committed to the separation of church and state, Europeans are not as absolute in maintaining the chasm. What is the difference in their approaches? And which approach do you believe Iraq will take as it moves toward democratization?

2. Buddhism, according to Amartya Sen, had a profound and widespread influence, far beyond its religious principles. Describe the intellectual link established between India and China, driven by Buddhism's agnosticism and its commitment to public discussion.

3. According to Goodstein, and notwithstanding conventional perceptions, religious fundamentalism is on the decline. What is the evidence of that? And what is the difference between fundamentalism and evangelism?

4. Mark Lilla observes that "the leading thinkers of the British and American Enlightenments hoped that life in a modern democratic order would shift the focus of Christianity from a faith-based reality to a reality-based faith." But Lilla also notes the trend today to search for a more ecstatic literalist religious experience. What are the dangers of this trend, in his view? Do you agree with him? If not, explain.

5. Cooperman reports on efforts for religious leaders on opposite ends of the left-right spectrum to find common ground, without conceding their own beliefs. What is the political significance of such efforts?

6. Why is it so important to democracy, as Nadine Strossen sees it, to maintain the strict separation of church and state?

II - C

The Wisdom of Modern Prophets

In this chapter we encounter the thoughts of several distinguished modern thinkers who concern themselves with an ethic for our time— in a world that is infinitely more interconnected and interdependent than ever before, where borders have become porous and information from the outside—from "the other"—part of every day reality. How can one with an absolute belief in one's faith live and thrive peacefully and equally in a world with others who may hold very different views with equal passion and conviction? Is democracy the answer? Or pluralism? Or Jonathan Sachs' concept, the dignity of difference?

The World House (Where Do We Go from Here)

Martin Luther King, Jr.

Some years ago a famous novelist died. Among his papers was found a list of suggested plots for future stories, the most prominently under-scored being this one: "A widely separated family inherits a house in which they have to live together." This is the great new problem of mankind. We have inherited a large house, a great "world house" in which we have to live together—black and white, Easterner and Westerner, Gentile and Jew, Catholic and Protestant, Moslem and Hindu—a family unduly separated in ideas, culture and interests, who, because we can never again live apart, must learn somehow to live with each other in peace.

However deeply American Negroes are caught in the struggle to be at last at home in our homeland of the United States, we cannot ignore the larger world house in which we are also dwellers. Equality with whites will not solve the problems of either whites or Negroes if it means equality in a world society stricken by poverty and in a uni-verse doomed to extinction by war.

All inhabitants of the globe are now neighbors. This world-wide neighborhood has been brought into being as a result of the modern scientific and technological revolutions. The world of today is vastly different from the world of just one hundred years ago. A century ago Thomas Edison had not yet invented the incandescent lamp to bring light to many dark places of the earth. The Wright brothers had not yet invented that fascinating mechanical bird that would spread its gigantic wings across the skies and soon dwarf distance and place time in the service of man. Einstein had not yet challenged an axiom and the theory of relativity had not yet been posited.

Human beings, searching a century ago as now for better under-standing, had no television, no radios, no telephones and no motion pictures through which to communicate. Medical science had not yet discovered the wonder drugs to end many dread plagues and diseases. One hundred years ago military men had not yet developed the terrifying weapons of warfare that we know today—not the bomber, an airborne fortress raining down death; nor napalm, that burner of all things and flesh in its path. A century ago there were no sky-scraping buildings to kiss the stars and no gargantuan bridges to span the waters. Science had not yet peered into the unfathomable ranges of interstellar space, nor had it penetrated oceanic depths. All these new inventions, these new ideas, these sometimes fascinating and sometimes frightening developments, came later. Most of them have come within the past sixty years, sometimes with agonizing slowness, more characteristically with bewildering speed, but always with enormous significance for our future.

The years ahead will see a continuation of the same dramatic developments. Physical science will carve new highways through the stratosphere. In a few years astronauts and cosmonauts will probably walk comfortably across the uncertain pathways of the moon. In two or three years it will be possible, because of the new supersonic jets, to fly from New York to London in two and one-half hours. In the years ahead medical science will greatly prolong the lives of men by finding a cure for cancer and deadly heart ailments. Automation and cybernation will make it possible for working people to have undreamed-of amounts of leisure time. All this is a dazzling picture of the furniture, the workshop, the spacious rooms, the new decorations and the architectural pattern of the large world house in which we are living.

Along with the scientific and technological revolution, we have also witnessed a world-wide freedom revolution over the last few decades. The present upsurge of the Negro people of the United States grows out of a deep and passionate determination to make freedom and equality a reality "here" and "now." In one sense the civil rights movement in the United States is a special American phenomenon which must be understood in the light of American history and dealt with in terms of the American situation. But on another and more important level, what is happening in the United States today is a significant part of a world development.

We live in a day, said the philosopher Alfred North Whitehead, "when civilization is shifting its basic outlook; a major turning point in history where the pre-suppositions on which society is structured are being analyzed, sharply challenged, and profoundly changed." What we are seeing now is a freedom explosion, the realization of "an idea whose time has come," to use Victor Hugo's phrase. The deep rumbling of discontent that we hear today is the thunder of disinherited masses, rising from dungeons of oppression to the bright hills of freedom. In one majestic chorus the rising masses are singing, in the words of our freedom song, "Ain't gonna let nobody turn us around." All over the world like a fever, freedom is spreading in the widest liberation movement in history. The great masses of people are determined to end the exploitation of their races and lands. They are awake and moving toward their goal like a tidal wave. You can hear them rumbling in every village street, on the docks, in the houses, among the students, in the churches and at political meetings. For several centuries the direction of history flowed from the nations and societies of Western Europe out into the rest of the world in "conquests" of various sorts. That period, the era of colonialism, is at an end. East is moving West. The earth is being redistributed. Yes, we are "shifting our basic outlooks." These developments should not surprise any student of history. Oppressed people cannot remain oppressed forever. The yearning for freedom eventually manifests itself. The Bible tells the thrilling story of how Moses stood in Pharaoh's court centuries ago and cried, "Let my people go." This was an opening chapter in a continuing story. The present struggle in the United States is a later chapter in the same story. Something within has reminded the Negro of his birthright of freedom, and something without has reminded him that it can be gained. Consciously or unconsciously, he has been caught up by the spirit of the times, and with his black brothers of Africa and his brown and yellow brothers in Asia, South America and the Caribbean, the United States Negro is moving with a sense of great urgency toward the promised land of racial justice.

Nothing could be more tragic than for men to live in these revolutionary times and fail to achieve the new attitudes and the new mental outlooks that the new situation demands. In Washington Irving's familiar story of Rip Van Winkle, the one thing that we usually remember is that Rip slept twenty years. There is another important point, however, that is almost always overlooked. It was the sign on the inn in the little town on the Hudson from which Rip departed and scaled the mountain for his long sleep. When he went up, the sign had a picture of King George III of England. When he came down, twenty years later, the sign had a picture of George Washington. As he looked at the picture of the first President of the United States, Rip was confused, flustered and lost. He knew not who Washington was. The most striking thing about this story is not that Rip slept twenty years, but that he slept through a revolution that would alter the course of human history.

One of the great liabilities of history is that all too many people fail to remain awake through great periods of social change. Every society has its protectors of the status quo and its fraternities of the indifferent who are notorious for sleeping through revolutions. But today our very survival depends on our ability to stay awake, to adjust to new ideas, to remain vigilant and to face the challenge of change. The large house in which we live demands that we transform this world-wide neighborhood into a world-wide brotherhood. Together we must learn to live as brothers or together we will be forced to perish as fools.

We must work passionately and indefatigably to bridge the gulf between our scientific progress and our moral progress. One of the great problems of mankind is that we suffer from a poverty of the spirit which stands in glaring contrast to our scientific and technological abundance. The richer we have become materially, the poorer we have become morally and spiritually.

Every man lives in two realms, the internal and the external. The internal is that realm of spiritual ends expressed in art, literature, morals and religion. The external is that complex of devices, techniques, mechanisms and instrumentalities by means of which we live. Our problem today is that we have allowed the internal to become lost in the external. We have allowed the means by which we live to outdistance the ends for which we live. So much of modern life can be summarized in that suggestive phrase of Thoreau: "Improved means to an unimproved end." This is the serious predicament, the deep and haunting problem, confronting modern man. Enlarged material powers spell enlarged peril if there is not proportionate growth of the soul. When the external of man's nature subjugates the internal, dark storm clouds begin to form.

Western civilization is particularly vulnerable at this moment, for our material abundance has brought us neither peace of mind nor serenity of spirit. An Asian writer has portrayed our dilemma in candid terms:

The large power blocs talk passionately of pursuing peace while expanding defense budgets that already bulge, enlarging already awesome armies and devising ever more devastating weapons. Call the roll of those who sing the glad tidings of peace and one's ears will be surprised by the responding sounds. The heads of all the nations issue clarion calls for peace, yet they come to the peace table accompanied by bands of brigands each bearing unsheathed swords.

The stages of history are replete with the chants and choruses of the conquerors of old who came killing in pursuit of peace. Alexander, Genghis Khan, Julius Caesar, Charlemagne and Napoleon were akin in seeking a peaceful world order, a world fashioned after their selfish conceptions of an ideal existence. Each sought a world at peace which would personify his egotistic dreams. Even within the life span of most of us, another megalomaniac strode across the world stage. He sent his blitzkrieg-bent legions blazing across Europe, bringing havoc and holocaust in his wake. There is grave irony in the fact that Hitler could come forth, following nakedly aggressive expansionist theories, and do it all in the name of peace. . . .

The United Nations is a gesture in the direction of nonviolence on a world scale. There, at least, states that oppose one another have sought to do so with words instead of with weapons. But true nonviolence is more than the absence of violence. It is the persistent and determined application of peaceable power to offenses against the community—in this case the world community. As the United Nations moves ahead with the giant tasks confronting it, I would hope that it would earnestly examine the uses of nonviolent direct action. . . .

These are revolutionary times. All over the globe men are revolting against old systems of exploitation and oppression, and out of the wombs of a frail world new systems of justice and equality are being born. The shirtless and barefoot people of the earth are rising up as never before. "The people who sat in darkness have seen a great light." We in the West must support these revolutions. It is a sad fact that, because of comfort, complacency, a morbid fear of Communism and our proneness to adjust to injustice, the Western nations that initiated so much of the revolutionary spirit of the modern world have now become the arch anti-revolutionaries. This has driven many to feel that only Marxism has the revolutionary spirit. Communism is a judgment on our failure to make democracy real and to follow through on the revolutions that we initiated. Our only hope today lies in our ability to recapture the revolutionary spirit and go out into a sometimes hostile world declaring eternal opposition to poverty, racism and militarism. With this powerful commitment we shall boldly challenge the status quo and unjust mores and thereby speed the day when "every valley shall be exalted, and every mountain and hill shall be made low: and the crooked shall be made straight and the rough places plain."

A genuine revolution of values means in the final analysis that our loyalties must become ecumenical rather than sectional. Every nation must now develop an overriding loyalty to mankind as a whole in order to preserve the best in their individual societies. This call for a world-wide fellowship that lifts neighborly concern beyond one's tribe, race, class and nation is in reality a call for an all-embracing and unconditional love for all men. This often misunderstood and misinterpreted concept has now become an absolute necessity for the survival of man. When I speak of love, I am speaking of that force which all the great religions have seen as the supreme unifying principle of life. Love is the key that unlocks the door which leads to ultimate reality. This Hindu-Moslem-Christian-Jewish-Buddhist belief about ultimate reality is beautifully summed up in the First Epistle of Saint John:

> *Let us love one another: for love is of God:*
> *and every one that loveth is born of God, and*
> *knoweth God. He that loveth not knoweth not*
> *God; for God is love. . . . If we love one another,*
> *God dwelleth in us, and his love is perfected in us.*

Let us hope that this spirit will become the order of the day. We can no longer afford to worship the God of hate or bow before the altar of retaliation. The oceans of history are made turbulent by the ever-rising tides of hate. History is cluttered with the wreckage of nations and individuals who pursued this self-defeating path of hate. As Arnold Toynbee once said in a speech: "Love is the ultimate force that makes for the saving choice of life and good against the damning choice of death and evil. Therefore the first hope in our inventory must be the hope that love is going to have the last word." We are now faced with the fact that tomorrow is today. We are confronted with the fierce urgency of *now*. In this unfolding conundrum of life and history there is such a thing as being too late. Procrastination is still the thief of time. Life often leaves us standing bare, naked and dejected with a lost opportunity. The "tide in the affairs of men" does not remain at the flood; it ebbs. We may cry out desperately for time to pause in her passage, but time is deaf to every plea and rushes on. Over the bleached bones and jumbled residues of numerous civilizations are written the pathetic words: "Too late." There is an invisible book of life that faithfully records our vigilance or our neglect. "The moving finger writes, and having writ moves on. . . ." We still have a choice today: nonviolent coexistence or violent co-annihilation. This may well be mankind's last chance to choose between chaos and community.

Balancing Religious Freedom and International Law

Robert F. Drinan, S.J.

In order to form coalitions, the essential thing that religious groups have to do is to make themselves more attractive to their neighbors. On a broader scale, religious groups must demonstrate that they are operating out of sincere love and not for narrow sectarian objectives. This is easy to say, but it must be remembered that the daily work of religious organizations is not by its nature designed to be attractive to those of another religion or of no religion.

Although the topic of securing religious freedom for everyone in the world seems overwhelming, there are some guidelines for persons involved in humanity's historic struggle to emancipate religious believers while not disadvantaging nonbelievers. I offer these thoughts for actors in religious bodies, governments, and nongovernmental agencies.

1. Religious Bodies

Persons working in religious organizations must urge believers to be restrained in any activity that might be perceived as an effort to impose their views on others or on governments. We must remember that adage that when a miracle occurs, no explanation for believers is necessary, while for nonbelievers no explanation is possible.

All religious bodies should recognize that the imposition of their beliefs on others goes against the sense of personal dignity and autonomy that is inculcated in the modern soul when international human rights are respected. The Declaration on Religious Freedom issued by the Second Vatican Council mentions this idea several times and in several ways. The essence of freedom of religion is "immunity from coercion" and the belief that a concept cannot be imparted "except by virtue of its own truth" (paragraph 1). Note 51 asserts that the declaration is "a final renouncement and repudiation by the Church of all means and measures of coercion in matters religious.

From *Can God and Caesar Coexist?* © 2004, Yale University Press, pp. 237–246. Reprinted with permission from Yale University Press.

All of the many references to religious freedom in the documents of the United Nations assume and imply that religious bodies will refrain from any measures that could be deemed to be coercive. The memory of "rice Christian"—the term applied to Asians who briefly espoused Christianity in order to obtain the food and comforts offered by missionaries—overshadows the topic of religious freedom in secular and sacred literature. The widespread practice of herding people into a faith by means approaching coercion has been repudiated by governments and by churches. At the same time, Muslim nations look upon anyone born into that religion as belonging irreversibly to that group.

Catholics were warned by the declarations of the Second Vatican Council that any hint of coercion in their dealings with Christians or non-Christians is inappropriate. Protestant sources have been saying the same thing for many years. In addition, the tenor of Catholic-Protestant relations has recently become more amicable than at any time since the Reformation. A clarification of international law on the full meaning of religious freedom would help both groups [Catholic and Protestant] to achieve the fullness of freedom that they want for themselves and for each other.

Catholics should find it particularly congenial to carry out the directives of the Universal Declaration of Human Rights, because Monsignor Angelo Roncalli, who subsequently became Pope John XXIII, collaborated in its preparation when he was the papal nuncio in Paris in 1948. Sean MacBride, human rights leader and Nobel laureate, affirmed that the future pope participated closely with René Cassin, the principal author of the Universal Declaration.

2. Government Actors

Governments have much to learn from international law's conferral of religious freedom on all ecclesiastical bodies. For centuries, local and national governments have been in the habit of using and misusing local religious groups for their own political objective, but those days should now be happily at an end.

The 1981 Universal Declaration on Religious Freedom is designed to curb the subordination of religion to the objectives of government. Article 4 of the declaration comments that all states "shall" prevent and eliminate discrimination on the grounds of religion or belief "in all fields of civil, economic, political, social and cultural life." Those broad terms were chosen to tell governments that checkerboard patterns in housing or business based on religious affiliation must be phased out.

The UN declaration makes it clear that no exclusion or preference based on religion or belief can be allowed. Its language is unmistakable: no nation can grant a higher or lower status to Christians, Muslims, Jews, or any other group on the sole basis of religion. Nor may a government exclude any person from any position in the nation on the basis of "religion or belief." Indeed, the ban extends to discrimination by "groups of persons or persons."

Many governments would hesitate to subscribe to the demands of the United Nations Declaration on Religious Freedom for fear that minority religious groups would press forward vigorously with demands for equality. Other nations would assert that as sovereign states they do not need the prodding of the declaration. But if the declaration ever became accepted, and certainly if it achieved the status of customary international law, there could be at least a minor revolution in the way governments look upon religious organizations.

Some observers will wonder whether the acceptance of the UN Declaration on Religious Freedom would make any difference. Would the war between Catholics and Protestants in Northern Ireland abate? Would the Kurds be treated differently? Would Christians in India be granted more tolerance? Would Christians in Sudan receive more acceptance? The only answer is that every law curbing discrimination and intolerance changes the world climate. Like civil rights in the United States, a world law protecting religious freedom would make discriminatory conduct less acceptable and eventually, it is hoped, make such conduct unthinkable.

Governments would be even less willing to agree to this reform if they believed that they would eventually be pressured to commit to treaty provisions allowing individual citizens to appeal an alleged denial of religious freedom to a UN tribunal. The spokespersons for some nations would protest the creation of a United Nations Commission on Religious Freedom on the basis that religious freedom, unlike the freedom of the press, defies definition or adjudication. Religion, they would argue, is so intertwined with culture and language that it cannot be realistically made the subject of a court decree. The argument has merit, but if there is to be an international right to faith, there will have to be some way of evaluating compliance.

Every nation has to search for its core identity through its legislature and its courts. The place of religion in the national culture is always a question of great concern, and every country has a unique history of its relation to religion. How a nation defines religious freedom is the end result of a very complicated process.

The United States is no exception. The U.S. Supreme Court coped with the issue in its 1952 6-3 ruling in *Zorach*. In 1948, in its 8-1 decision in *McCollum*, the Court had banned classes in religion for students in public schools, even when the students had the written permission of their parents. The national protest over this decision had been vehement. In *Zorach*, the Supreme Court was called upon to rule on the constitutionality of religious education conducted by public schools but held off school premises. The Supreme Court allowed this arrangement, stating in a decision written by Justice William Douglas that "we are a religious people whose institutions presuppose the existence of a supreme being." If other nations felt the same way, they would theoretically be prepared to accept a worldwide monitor to guarantee that their people could perpetuate their status as a "religious people."

3. Nongovernmental Actors

A third group of spokespersons is the rapidly growing community of nongovernmental organizations (NGOs) devoted to human rights. The scope of involvement and the intensity of devotion of this new community are amazing. NGOs fight for the rights of women, children, refugees, the disabled, and other groups of victims. They were omnipresent at the United Nations World Conference on Human Rights in Vienna in 1993, and since then they have evidenced even greater levels of involvement and influence.

These groups are so committed to their goals that it is not appropriate to fault them. It does seem, however, that their interest in religious freedom has not developed in the same way as their attention to other issues. This is quite understandable, inasmuch as there is not yet a United Nations covenant on religious freedom, only a declaration. At the same time, the neglect of religious freedom pulls apart the seamless garment of which all human rights are part. If nations are not placed under pressure for the mishandling of religious freedom, they may be less likely to comply with their duties under other pledges solemnly made to the United Nations. In addition, it must be noted that if religious dissidents are allowed to speak out and act on behalf of human rights, a whole new army of friends of human rights will have been created.

Some of the most vigorous NGOs devoted to human rights are affiliated with Jewish organizations. From the World Jewish Congress down to the local level, Jewish-affiliated NGOs have led the way. These groups were uniquely successful in their efforts to bring relief to the 3 million Soviet Jews, half or more of whom were finally allowed to emigrate to the United States, Israel, and elsewhere.

There are probably no Christian human rights organizations as influential as those of Jewish origin. Christian groups have depended on an ever-broader array of NGOs devoted to human rights. However, a coalition of Jewish and Christian organizations devoted to the enlargement of freedom could be uniquely effective. Christians have the additional motive of seeking to offer atonement for the Holocaust, which occurred in Christian countries.

People of faith tend to see the will of God in human events. At the same time, many religious people want to take up secular, even violent means to stop evil things from harming religious institutions. The approval of violent means by the Christian Church has at times been so pervasive that before the Middle Ages, the Church helped to devise seven conditions for a "just" war. But this thinking is now possibly obsolete.

People of faith started the Crusades and other "holy wars" to protect the Church. Today Catholics feel chagrin and guilt for many actions taken through the centuries to protect and extend the Church. Pope John Paul II has publicly apologized for some eighty acts of the Church through the centuries. Some of those mistakes were made in the name of advancing the faith or curbing the "infidels." Many of them were designed to, and did, deny or blunt the victims' religious freedom.

The Catholics, like all Christians, have altered in many ways their ideas about what actions to advance the faith are legitimate. But despite this change in Christian attitude, past misdeeds linger in the history books and in the living and continuing memory of millions of people who regard the acts as indefensible. Of course, this history also affects the attitudes of the over 1 billion Catholics living everywhere in the world who ask how their church could ever have used the power of Caesar to advance the objectives of God. Of course, Protestants are also forced to reconcile the fact that their religion has sometimes used similar tactics. In the end, wars against heretics and comparable measures have left today's Christians stunned, repentant, and determined to change their ways.

Today it is governments who are slaying people who follow religions deemed to be enemies. It was the government in El Salvador that killed Archbishop Oscar Romero, six Jesuit professors, and four American churchwomen. It was the governments in Berlin, Moscow, and Beijing that killed countless persons of faith deemed to be the enemies of the state.

Can more treaties and more emphasis on the necessity of religious freedom change the dreadful pattern that has historically been followed? The framers of the United Nations Declaration on Religious Freedom and all the most idealistic and humanitarian persons since the end of World War II have placed their confidence in the rule of law, the inviolability of human rights, and the exaltation of religious freedom as the best ways to restore and preserve civilization. Their words have been translated into world law binding on all 191 member states of the United Nations. The governments of these countries have made solemn pledges to enforce those moral concepts in their own laws.

One of the most urgent of all those objectives, the advancement of religious freedom, has received disappointingly little attention by the UN's member states and even by the religious bodies it was designed to protect. History may well record that one of the greatest disappointments in the second half of the twentieth century was the neglect and the silence that governments and religious organizations extended to the efforts of the United Nations to preserve and enlarge religious freedom.

Of course, many religious groups have actively sought to guarantee religious freedom to everyone in the world. One example is the Parliament of World Religions, held in August 1993, which brought 6,500 individuals to Chicago from fifty-six nations and from nearly all the world's major religions. The parliament's "Declaration Towards a Global Ethic" echoed the sentiments of the first World Parliament of Religion, held in Chicago in 1893.

The final statement in the parliament's declaration is not expressly theistic, but rather embraces concepts of human dignity that are applicable to a wide range of beliefs. Its statement on the Golden Rule is as follows: "There is a principle which is found and has persisted in many religious and ethical traditions of human kind for thousands of years: What you do not wish done to yourself, do not do to others! Or in positive terms: What you wish done to yourself, do to others!" This should be the irrevocable, unconditional norm for all areas of life, for families and communities, for races, nations and religions.

Some people may feel that this statement is too general to be particularly helpful in efforts to resolve awful dilemmas surrounded by agonizing problems. But at least it is a global effort to bring religious personages of all backgrounds together and make a pledge to live by the Golden Rule.

Will there ever be an age when God and Caesar can coexist in peace? Law is a feeble instrument to bring about that laudable objective. If law is to be effective, it must be joined with love—and love for others is at the core of every religion and every code of conduct.

Buddhism, Asian Values, and Democracy

Dalai Lama

While democratic aspirations may be manifested in different ways, some universal principles lie at the heart of any democratic society—representative government (established through free and fair elections), the rule of law and accountability (as enforced by an independent judiciary), and freedom of speech (as exemplified by an uncensored press). Democracy, however, is about much more than these formal institutions; it is about genuine freedom and the empowerment of the individual. I am neither an expert in political science nor an authority on democracy and the rule of law. Rather, I am a simple Buddhist monk, educated and trained in our ancient, traditional ways. Nonetheless, my life-long study of Buddhism and my involvement in the Tibetan people's nonviolent struggle for freedom have given me some insights that I would like to discuss.

As a Buddhist monk, I do not find alien the concept and practice of democracy. At the heart of Buddhism lies the idea that the potential for awakening and perfection is present in every human being and that realizing this potential is a matter of personal effort. The Buddha proclaimed that each individual is a master of his or her own destiny, highlighting the capacity that each person has to attain enlightenment. In this sense, the Buddhist worldview recognizes the fundamental sameness of all human beings. Like Buddhism, modern democracy is based on the principle that all human beings are essentially equal, and that each of us has an equal right to life, liberty, and happiness. Whether we are rich or poor, educated or uneducated, a follower of one religion or another, each of us is a human being. Not only do we desire happiness and seek to avoid suffering, but each of us also has an equal right to pursue these goals. Thus not only are Buddhism and democracy compatible, they are rooted in a common understanding of the equality and potential of every individual.

From Bstan-dzin-rgya-mtsho, Dalai Lama XIV. "Buddhism, Asian Values, and Democracy." *Journal of Democracy* 10:1 (1999), 3–7. © National Endowment For Democracy and The Johns Hopkins University Press. Reprinted with permission of The Johns Hopkins University Press.

As for democracy as a procedure of decision-making, we find again in the Buddhist tradition a certain recognition of the need for consensus. For example, the Buddhist monastic order has a long history of basing major decisions affecting the lives of individual monks on collective discourse. In fact, strictly speaking, every rite concerning the maintenance of monastic practice must be performed with a congregation of at least four monks. Thus one could say that the Vinaya rules of discipline that govern the behavior and life of the Buddhist monastic community are in keeping with democratic traditions. In theory at least, even the teachings of the Buddha can be altered under certain circumstances by a congregation of a certain number of ordained monks.

As human beings, we all seek to live in a society in which we can express ourselves freely and strive to be the best we can be. At the same time, pursuing one's own fulfillment at the expense of others would lead to chaos and anarchy. What is required, then, is a system whereby the interests of the individual are balanced with the wider well being of the community at-large. For this reason, I feel it is necessary to develop a sense of universal responsibility, a deep concern for all human beings, irrespective of religion, color, gender, or nationality. If we adopt a self-centered approach to life and constantly try to use others to advance our own interests, we may gain temporary benefits, but in the long run happiness will elude us. Instead, we must learn to work not just for our own individual selves, but for the benefit of all mankind.

While it is true that no system of government is perfect, democracy is the closest to our essential human nature and allows us the greatest opportunity to cultivate a sense of universal responsibility. As a Buddhist, I strongly believe in a humane approach to democracy, an approach that recognizes the importance of the individual without sacrificing a sense of responsibility toward all humanity. Buddhists emphasize the potential of the individual, but we also believe that the purpose of a meaningful life is to serve others.

Many nations consider respect for the individual's civil and political rights to be the most important aspect of democracy. Other countries, especially in the developing world, see the rights of the society—particularly the right to economic development—as overriding the rights of the individual. I believe that economic advancement and respect for individual rights are closely linked. A society cannot fully maximize its economic advantage without granting its people individual civil and political rights. At the same time, these freedoms are diminished if the basic necessities of life are not met.

Some Asian leaders say that democracy and the freedoms that come with it are exclusive products of Western civilization. Asian values, they contend, are significantly different from, if not diametrically opposed to, democracy. They argue that Asian cultures emphasize order, duty and stability, while the emphasis of Western democracies on individual rights and liberties undermines those values. They suggest that Asians have fundamentally different needs in terms of personal and social fulfillment. I do not share this viewpoint.

It is my fundamental belief that all human beings share the same basic aspirations: We all want happiness and we all experience suffering. Like Americans, Europeans, and the rest of the world, Asians wish to live life to its fullest, to better themselves and the lives of their loved ones. India, the birthplace of Mahatma Gandhi and the concept of *ahimsa*, or nonviolence, is an excellent example of an Asian country devoted to a democratic form of government. India demonstrates that democracy can sink strong roots outside the Western world. Similarly, our brothers and sisters in Burma, Indonesia, and China are courageously raising their voices together in the call for equality, freedom, and democracy.

The fact that democratic reforms are on the rise around the globe, from the Czech Republic to Mongolia, and from South Africa to Taiwan, is testimony to the strength of the ideals that democracy embodies. As more and more people gain awareness of their individual potential, the number of people seeking to express themselves through a democratic system grows. These global trends illustrate the universality of the desire for a form of government that respects human rights and the rule of law.

The Dignity of Difference

Jonathan Sacks

For the foreseeable future, the fate of liberty will be in American hands. I say this consciously as a European. With or against its will, the United States has been drawn into a series of global conflicts, some economic, others political, yet others religious, all in some way interrelated and mutually reinforcing. These are difficult for the modern mind—with its tendency to compartmentalize thought into separate, self-enclosed disciplines—to wrestle with. At such times, an outsider's perspective may be helpful, especially one who, after long reflection, has come to see the American project as the single most successful answer to humanity's deepest question: how to turn our post-Babel differences into a source of blessing rather than conflict.

The closest analogy to the turmoil of the twenty-first century is seventeenth-century Europe, out of which the United States was ultimately born. Then as now, religious wars, intertwined with political and economic considerations, threatened the future of the West. The Reformation, the invention of printing and the breakdown of empire led to a period of unrest and uncertainty from which a new order eventually emerged. We are living through a period with the same conflictual forces—a new religiosity, a revolution in communications technology, and the collapse of an overarching political structure. But the context has changed, the participants are different and the stakes—the human capacity for destruction—immeasurably higher.

We will need all the wisdom we can find. One such source is the Jewish tradition, from which in their different ways Christianity, Islam and (not least) American politics drew inspiration. What makes that tradition particularly interesting now (and believers alike) is that biblical monotheism was humanity's first attempt to think globally, to confront issues of economic inequality, environmental destruction, information

From *The Dignity of Difference* by Jonathan Sacks, pp. ix–xi, 200–203. © Continuum, London: 2002. Reprinted by permission of The Continuum International Publishing Group.

technology and human dignity, war and the pursuit of peace. The book of Genesis was the first to see all humankind as bound by a universal covenant, and yet to acknowledge the legitimacy of profound religious and cultural differences. Historic challenges require historic resources and the sweep of large imagination. That is why, in the great debates about globalisation, the clash of civilizations and the campaign against terror, insight is to be gained from a fresh encounter with the Hebrew Bible, the foundational text of Western ethics and spirituality.

I am repeatedly struck, in my visits to North America and my reading of its literature, by its self-renewing energy. It has emerged, after a period of self-doubt, as the world's sole superpower, dominating the international landscape but without the hubris that has affected and corrupted other colossi of the past. Much of that, I suspect, has come from its own political narrative, articulated in presidential inaugurals from Washington to George W. Bush, which to an outsider read like nothing so much as an extended commentary to the Hebrew Bible, with its themes of covenant, the journey to a promised land, care for 'the exile and the stranger,' and the knowledge, as John F. Kennedy put it, that 'the rights of man come not from the generosity of the state but from the hand of God.' The United States has kept what Europe has largely lost; its faith, its sense of 'one nation under God,' and most importantly its ethical clarity, its ability to see the difference between good and evil, even when good involves self-restraint and evil is hidden under the cloak of religious fervour. We will need these things in the years to come.

My argument, however, is that the vocabulary that served America so well in the past is inadequate to the challenge of the future. The United States developed two ideas to allow people of different traditions to live peaceably together: the First Amendment's separation of church and state, and Horace Kallen's early twentieth-century concept, pluralism. What makes these insufficient is that they work for a society, not the world. They presuppose an overarching civil power to keep the peace. They are also secular and essentially *de facto*. They acknowledge, rather than celebrate, diversity. Something stronger will be needed if different nations, faiths and cultures are to live together in a world with no global governance, in an age of extreme and counter-modern religiosity. The idea I propound is the dignity of difference. This is not, like pluralism, a secular doctrine; nor is it, like the separation of church and state, an attempt to place limits on religion, however wise those limits are. It is instead a way of locating the celebration of diversity at the very heart of the monotheistic imagination.

I have given it a secular logic as well—it underlies both biodiversity (the natural environment) and economic exchange (the social environment). But my primary aim has been to suggest a new paradigm for our complex, interconnected world, in such a way that, the more passionately we feel our religious commitments, the more space we make for those not like us. I offer it not only as an analysis of some difficult global challenges but also as a prayer, in which I invite other to join, for peace in a world in which the risk and cost of war have become too high. We will need a new vision if we are to find another way.

There is nothing relativist about the idea of the dignity of difference. It is based on the radical transcendence of God from the created universe, with its astonishing diversity of live forms—all of which, as we now know through genetic research, derive from a single source—and from the multiple languages and cultures through which we, as meaning-seeking beings, have attempted to understand the totality of existence. Just as the human situation would be impoverished and unsustainable if we were to eliminate all life forms except our own, so it would be reduced and fatally compromised if we were to eliminate all cultural, civilizational and religious forms except our own. The idea that we fulfil God's will by waging war against the infidel, or converting the heathen, so that all humanity shares the same faith is an idea that—as I have tried to argue—owes much to the concept of empire and little to the heritage of Abraham, which Jews, Christians and Muslims claim as their own. It was not until the Abrahamic faith came into contact with Greek and Roman imperialism that it developed into an aspiration to conquer or convert the world, and we must abandon it if we are to save ourselves from mutual destruction. To repeat my formulation in an earlier chapter: fundamentalism, like imperialism, is the attempt to impose a single truth on a plural world. It is the Tower of Babel of our time.

The test of faith is whether I can make space for difference. Can I recognize God's image in someone who is not in my image, whose language, faith ideals, are different from mine? If I cannot, then I have made God in my image instead of allowing him to remake me in his. Can Israeli make space for Palestinian, and Palestinian for Israeli? Can Muslims, Hindus, Sikhs, Confucians, Orthodox, Catholics, and Protestants make space for one another in India, Sri Lanka, Chechnya, Kosovo and the dozens of other places in which different ethnic and religious groups exist in close proximity? Can we create a paradigm shift through which we come to recognize that we are enlarged, not diminished, by difference, just as we are enlarged, not diminished by the 6,000 languages that exist today, each with its unique sensibilities, art forms and literary expressions? This is not the cosmopolitanism of those who belong nowhere, but the deep human understanding that passes between people who, knowing how important their attachments are to them, understand how deeply someone else's different attachments matter to them also.

* * *

With this I return to a concept that has underlain much of what I have argued—the concept of *covenant*. Initially a form of treaty between neighbouring powers in the ancient Near East, it became, in the Hebrew Bible, a–even the–central form of relationship, laden with religious and moral significance. Covenant is an answer to the most fundamental question in the evolution of societies: How can we establish relationships secure enough to become the basis of co-operation, without the use economic, political, or military power? The use of power is ruled out by the requirement of human dignity. If you and I are linked because, one way or another, I can force you to do what I want, then I have secured my freedom at the cost of yours. I have asserted my humanity by denying yours. Covenant is the attempt to create partnership without dominance or submission. It exists because of one extraordinary feature of language. We can use words to place ourselves under obligation. The great Oxford philosopher J. L. Austin called this 'performative utterance'. Covenant occurs when two individuals or groups, differing perhaps in power, but each acknowledging the integrity and sovereignty of the other, pledge themselves in mutual loyalty to achieve together what neither can achieve alone. Covenant is the use of language to create a bond of trust through the word given, the word received, the word honoured in mutual fidelity.

A covenant is not a contract. It differs in three respects. It is not limited to specific conditions and circumstances. It is open-ended and long-lasting. And it is not based on the idea of two individuals, otherwise unconnected, pursuing personal advantage. It is about the 'We' that gives identity to the 'I'. There is a place for contracts, but covenants are prior and more fundamental. They form the matrix of mutuality within which contractual relationships can exist. As Philip Selznick notes:

Every genuine covenant restates and reaffirms the basic feature of morality: deference to a source of judgement beyond autonomous will; constructive self-regard; concern for the well-being of others. At the same time, it establishes the principle of a *particular* way of life . . . It is not an abstract morality.[1]

What makes covenant a concept for our time is that it affirms the dignity of difference. The great covenantal relationships—between God and mankind, between man and woman in marriage, between members of community of citizens of society—exist because both parties recognize that 'it is not good for man to be alone'. God cannot redeem the world without human participation; humanity cannot redeem the world without recognition of the divine. Man alone, and woman alone, cannot bring new life into the world. Members and citizens alone cannot sustain themselves, let alone establish a frame-work of collaborative action and to preserve that difference, even as we come together to bring our several gifts to the common good. They are brought into being because of the non-zero-sumness of relationship and interaction.

Covenants—because they are relational, not ontological—are inherently pluralistic. I have one kind of relationship with my parents, another with my spouse, others with my children, yet others with friends, neighbours, members of my faith, fellow citizens of my country, and with human beings wherever they suffer and need my help. None of these is exclusive. It is of the nature of real life, as opposed to philosophical abstraction, that we have many commit-ments and that they may, at times, conflict. But that is not inherently tragic, though it may give rise to regret, even grief. Pluralism is a form of hope, because it is founded in the understanding that pre-cisely because we are different, each of us has something unique to contribute to the shared project of which we are a part. In the short term, our desires and needs may clash; but the very realization that difference is a source of blessing leads us to seek mediation, conflict resolution, conciliation and peace—the peace that is predicated on diversity, not on uniformity.

Endnote

[1] Phillip Selznick, *The Moral Commonwealth*, (Berkeley, CA: University of California Press, 1994), p. 480.

Grounding Democracy in Reverence for Life: A View from Judaism

Irving Greenberg

The Value of Limitations

There is . . . [a] crucial element in covenant that links it to democracy. The essence of covenant lies in setting limits. For God to enter into covenant, God must self-limit. The Kabbalah argues that the very act of creation is a form of self-limitation. The laws of nature are the first steps of covenant. Creation begins with God's self-limiting to make the universe possible. Otherwise, the divine plenitude would fill the world and there would be no room for existence. The next covenantal step comes when God further accepts the boundaries and guidelines of covenant to make room for human dignity.

What does it mean when we say that entering into the covenant imposes limits on God? One implication is that God will not force or coerce humans to be good. That is the lesson of the flood story in the Book of Genesis. In the aftermath, God renounces divine power to override nature, promising never again to attempt to force people to be good. The Divine also renounces the alternative possibility of programming people to be good. Thus God fundamentally accepts human freedom. Freedom is built on the right to do wrong. In order to do right, you do not need freedom. But God prefers achieving the dignified free creature (the human) over the guarantee of that creature doing the right thing. The divine goal in creating and sustaining the image of God is to create a creature that is free, independent and responsible.

The covenantal commitment shows that God would accept disobedience and failure rather than insist on perfection by coercion. This further implies that the Divine treats humans as truly equal and truly unique, passing up the opportunity to program humans to do the right thing. The implication of this model for democracy is that it is not enough to establish majority rule. One needs to allow for the independent dignity of the others; true democracy demands minority rights, not just majority power.

© *Religions in Dialogue*, Alan Race and Ingrid Shafer, 2002, Ashgate Publishing Company, UK, pp. 32–35.

Divine self-limitation implies the importance of making room for the existence of another. The covenantal partner must listen to the other. It follows that a religiously guided democracy must embrace the right to be heard. The mere fact that an infinitely valuable creature is speaking, one who is equal to you, means that I have the right to speak. But what if I am wrong? If I am equal, then you may try to persuade me to think otherwise than I do. However, elemental respect for my equality means that I have the right to speak and to be heard—even if I am wrong.

All of this sounds lovely and ideal, but the historical records of the monotheistic religions show little past affinity for democracy. What went wrong? As participants in the process of covenant, all religions, all people, are involved in historical temporality. They start from the real world as it is; they become implicated in all the inequalities and injustices of the world. But in trying to improve the world, religions have too often gone out of control. They have failed to learn the lesson that the Divine works within limits out of respect for humans. Therefore human beings—even when they uphold divine religion—must work within limits also.

The lack of limits has been the key to religious misbehaviour. As democracy teaches that there are limits so that one should not coerce the minority, so religion should have understood the same message. If the image of God is truly respected, if the principle of covenant is truly obeyed, then one would accept bad behaviour rather then force good behaviour. Out of respect for human freedom one tries to educate and persuade, not to coerce. Unfortunately, the classic monotheistic religions, in the name of God and in the name of their own teachings, have insisted on having the right to enforce the faith. Often this has meant demanding the right to pressure, or even to kill, in order to uphold that faith. Absolute power in the name of God always goes wrong; it constantly slides into abuse of the other and betrayal of the principle of human dignity. In short, religions have historically acted badly because they failed to imitate God's nature, especially God's self-limitation.

Limitation and Religious Pluralism

The essence of pluralism, which is inescapably built into democracy, is that I may believe that I have the whole truth but I also acknowledge the limits of my viewpoint. Pluralism is not relativism. Pluralism does not entail, as the popular misunderstanding has it, that anything goes, that one should never make judgments. In the practice of pluralism, I do affirm my own truth. Therefore my truth may contradict, challenge or critique those views which I believe to be wrong. But, in democracy, I accept that there are limits to my understanding of truth. Therefore I cannot force others to follow my truth. Pluralism is an absolutism that has learned its own limitations. Any group ideology or faith that recognizes its own limitations will make room for others. Consequently, it will self-limit. It will renounce coercion and violence towards the other. That limit makes it healthy and functional.

If God did not self-limit, existence could not exist. Religious truth that has no limits will not let anyone else exist. What is the proper religious limitation? At the minimum, it is that I recognize my religion as absolute truth, but I still make room for other religions. Or I may come to a deeper insight: that my faith has not exhausted the divine truth. Other religions may have other elements beyond mine, or they may have the same elements as mine does. The third possibility is that perhaps I witness the truth, the whole truth, nothing but the truth, but still God has other truths or additional revelations for other people. This may stem from the fact that God wants to include others in this partnership for *tikkun olam* or simply because God desires to reach others.

Even if a religion could finally articulate 100 per cent of the truth, there are so many polarities in these truths. For example, take love and justice. If one religion is focused primarily on love, then it cannot easily hold the other pole, justice, in tandem as well as some other faith might. If a religion is all love, it cannot do justice to justice. Alternatively, if a religion is 100 per cent focused on justice, it cannot do justice to love. Therefore pluralism teaches that we must make room for other religions that have different bounds. These are just examples of some of the ways in which pluralist self-limiting religion will understand itself.

Let me speak more personally now. My faith was challenged and broken by an encounter with the Holocaust. For a long time I dreamed that this tragedy had broken me, but that perhaps someday I would return to the wholeness of the original truth—my original experience of unfailing divine presence. I came to see later that the essence of covenant is that no truth is unbroken. The process of limitation—brokenness is another word for limitation—is the essence of the divine capacity to address human beings. God must in some sense limit, restrict, restrain—and therefore the divine word must, in some sense, break or shrink in order to communicate the truth. God cannot do full justice to God's own plenitude once the Divine gets involved with human beings. Therefore the truth is that all truths, even eternal truths, are momentary truths. What renders eternal truth eternal is that it speaks in many moments, as against a truth that has a half-life of one moment or part of a moment.

Democracy teaches us to acknowledge our limitations and to recognize the presence of many other worthy people in public life. God, too, has many messengers. Pluralism leads me to recognize that the overflowing love of the Divine is never exhausted. My presence, my mind my revelation, no matter how great, cannot exhaust infinity. Therefore, there must be room for other messages that do not supersede mine, or messengers who are not inferior to mine. Each messenger recognizes that he or she does not own God exclusively. The notion of covenant implies that God enters into loving partnership with this particular group. But God can do so again and again. Each covenantal group needs teachers and role models to carry out its task.

Good ideas alone, no matter how good they are, do not work unless they are implemented in the real world. Therefore, one needs multiple role models and one should consequently welcome the other covenant groups as such. Those seeking to affect the world for the good come to see that the obstacles are vast and the suffering is great. As the problems are beyond the capacity of any single group or religion or tradition to resolve, everyone should welcome co-workers. One should not be jealous and deny or reject the dignity and values of other faiths. What went wrong with religion is that religious leaders were so inspired by their own greatness that they could not conceive of anybody else being able to accomplish the goal. Therefore, in the end, the religious prayer was twisted into demanding that *our* will be done. If we seek that God's will be done, then why would we not welcome, rather then reject, the fact that God called others to be messengers and co-workers and teachers in this process?

The strength of the democratic system is that it creates a framework where both intrinsic dignity and limits exist. In a democracy, failures—which are endemic and implicit in all human activity—can be criticized and corrected. The great breakthrough of democracy is that the failures are limited by the system, for others are free to correct and challenge. They are equal and possess the right to try to reform. Democracy provides the framework that maximizes the chance of an outcome that plays off the strengths of all. Democracy offers the vision of respecting the equality and dignity of others so that freedom and mutual respect are continuously advanced. This is the new calling to our future religions: to affirm and to function in this democratic way in our lifetime and for the future.

Ethics and Politics

Mohammed Arkoun

The concept of a moral totality validated entirely by divine teaching (Qur'an, hadith) continues to dominate contemporary Islamic discourse and has even assumed an unprecedented public dimension, thanks to the multiplier effect of the media. But in terms of social psychology, this ethical-ideological vision feeds a social imaginary much more than it nourishes a sort of ethical reasoning capable of careful discernment and value critique. I thus come back to what I have already said about politics: The gulf becomes ever wider between the imaginary but obsessive representation of the prophetic model and the concrete behavior of individuals subject to the interplay of more and more severe economic, social, and political constraints. Material modernity plays a devastating role. For even the most humble, it prescribes norms of consumption, costly necessities, criteria for entry into a universally desired mode of existence. It engages all the energies and strategies of conduct in a direction that is counter to traditional morality, which is based in the subsistence economy. Structural changes affect social relationships, value hierarchies, and "moral" definitions without the agents knowing what is happening because there is scarcely any sociological, psychological, or philosophical analysis to take account of these generalized processes.

A study of money-driven corruption in contemporary Muslim societies would overturn the image of the Islamic model enjoying favor in idealistic, nostalgic discourse. In such countries there is illegal dealing even in passports for the pilgrimage to Mecca. Faced with the leadenness and shortcomings of administration and the extreme remoteness of the state, citizens have recourse to a parallel system of exchanging services with compensation in either money or favors. Obtaining visas, housing, plane tickets, commercial licenses, enrollment in a school, construction materials, places in line to buy automobiles or rare machines—all the requirements of professional and daily life are subject to tough and lucrative negotiation.

The code of honor and the symbolic capital that conferred a divine, religious, disinterested meaning to all exchanges effected at all levels of social and economic life lie far in the past. The brutal eruption of material modernity (industrialization, agrarian reform, urbanization, uprooting of rural populations, new consumption needs, travel, communication, and so on) has disrupted traditional solidarities and replaced values of fidelity, loyalty, mutual assistance, unconditional solidarity, constancy, generosity; hospitality, and respect for promises, human dignity, and the property of others with strategies for getting rich quickly, for social and economic ascent, and for gaining power. The old values everywhere sustained the ethos of societies where Islam is widespread and brought spiritual gain by focusing all questions of moral conduct on the absoluteness of God. This is true for Arabia itself, where Islam was born, and it can be verified in the other Islamized countries, from Indonesia to Morocco, from Turkey to Senegal.

Old and deeply rooted in individual habit as it is, this ethos, the cement of traditional societies, is no longer externalized except as militant energy in the so-called Islamist movements. That is why it is difficult to analyze with precision the very ambiguous contents of the discourse and behavior of these movements. While the political objective is clear and predominant, the emphasis on ethical and religious motives is never absent. There is surely an investment of a spiritual energy of ethical-religious origin in the revolutionary accomplishments of these movements.

That consideration poses the problem of ethical judgment in contemporary Muslim societies: Using Islamic criteria, can we attribute a moral and religious status to the acts termed "revolutionary" by the agents and their superiors, "terrorist" by the victims? The Muslim jurist-theologians of the period of ijtihad would have posed the question in these same terms and in this perspective. I do not see it raised anywhere in our time.

Is this to say that the criterion of efficiency, of pragmatic action, has definitively replaced, as it has in the West, that which al-Ghazali called "the balance of moral action," mizän at- 'amal? For sure, the "scientific" appraisal of the circumstances, the conditions for production, of an act tend everywhere to cause the suspension of moral judgment or its complete elimination. This tendency is a sign of our culture and our so-called modern civilization. It is a blindspot of intellectual modernity; In the case of Muslim societies, the abyss is even greater between the multiplication and extension of violent behaviors and the opportunities remaining for intellectuals to counterbalance semantic disorder and the rout of thought. Western democracies provide lots of free space where critical thought and artistic creativity can at least lay stepping stones toward new beginnings of reflection, of knowledge, and of moral, political, and cognitive codes. Moreover, scientific and technological research continually modify the material and moral conditions in which these societies produce their existence. These simultaneous activities have great capacity to integrate and direct. There is nothing equivalent to these processes in contemporary Muslim societies. The Muslim societies import the most complex technological materiel, buy the most sophisticated armaments, and install high-performance laboratories, but at the same time governments exercise such rigorous ideological control that all these instruments of scientific modernity have little perceptible effect on mentalities or even on reflective thought. The capacity to integrate and to progress is transformed into an agent of disintegration and semantic detour.

Some may find this picture of morality and politics in the Islamic world a bit pessimistic or extreme. In fact, I have tried to undertake a diagnosis much more than to give an exhaustive description of all the manifestations and expressions of ethics and politics. In contrast, the Orientalist approach to Muslim societies expressly forgoes diagnosis, because Orientalists decline to interfere in questions that do not concern them as citizens of Western societies.

The Muslim intellectual must today fight on two fronts: one against social science as practiced by Orientalism in a disengaged, narrative, descriptive style; the other against the offensive/defensive apologia of Muslims who compensate for repeated attacks on the "authenticity" and the "identity" of the Islamic personality with dogmatic affirmations and self-confirming discourse. And beyond these two obstacles, always present but at least identifiable, the Muslim intellectual must contribute through the Islamic example to an even more fundamental diagnosis, especially regarding questions of ethics and politics: 'What are the blindspots, the failings, the non sequiturs, the alienating constraints, the recurrent weaknesses of modernity? Protest must reach every form of activity, every point of intervention, every logical structure. From Hegel to Nietzsche, Enlightenment thought was invoked as the opposite of myth in an effort to escape the clutches of religious dogma; at the same time that reason performed this "liberating" critique, it also fell back into a nostalgic celebration of the origins of civilization, especially the

Greek polis and the first Christian communities, which were the equivalent of the "Pious Elders" among the Muslims.

Scholars get beyond Enlightenment thought by integrating myth—hence the accumulated symbolic capital carried and maintained by religion—into the cognitive activity of reason. The comparative history of religion, conducted within this perspective, furnishes a particularly fertile ground for the elaboration of new kinds of rationality. It goes without saying that forms of religious expression cannot be detached from symbolic and artistic creativity. It is not a matter of extending indefinitely the horizons of meaning open to the scrutiny of reason. Instead of exhausting ourselves in an effort to reclaim contingent values tied to abandoned forms of culture and bygone systems of civilization, scholars today must propose new opportunities for the emancipation, exaltation, and mastery of human existence and for the thought and action of men and women.[1]

Endnote

[1] I corrected the proofs of this chapter on January 22, 1991, while the Gulf War was taking so many lives and raising so many passions and so much indignation everywhere in the world. I originally wrote the chapter in July 1990, before the outbreak of the crisis in the Gulf. I nonetheless stick with my critical analysis and my refusal of militant forms of discourse from whatever source. I feel only a need to further radicalize that which I have already written by adding a critique of "Western" reason, which is so sure of itself and of the right that it intends to make prevail even though its material and technological hegemony has rendered obsolete, bypassed, and useless all ethical considerations. I have not come across many "Western" intellectuals who write or speak, as they should, of the failings of such reason since 1945 and of the even more tragic failings that will surely be apparent after the Gulf War I fear, in fact, that we are returning very quickly to the status quo ante of "international order."

The Idea of Democratic
Religious Government

Abdolkarim Soroush

We are approaching the end of our discussion, and a brief summary is in order. This essay originated in the question of the possibility of combining democracy and religion; but it went on to articulate their affinity and need for each other. Notions of liberty, faith, dynamism of religious understanding, and rationality of worldly affairs were evoked to attest to the possibility, even the necessity, of such an auspicious reconciliation. Religious morality would be the guarantor of a democracy, where the rights of the faithful to adopt a divine religion would not vitiate the democratic, earthly, and rational nature of the religious government. A distinction between democracy and the liberal philosophy helped demonstrate that the convictions of the faithful do not impede religious tolerance. Recognizing the primacy of general epistemological and theological axioms over the specifics of religious law determined the status of each; the emphasis on the necessity of maintaining the equilibrium between the religious and extrareligious domain illustrated the role of rationality in the domain of religion and took the critique of democratic religiosity out of the jurisdiction of religious law. At the same time, legal discipline was recognized as a contributing factor in religious democracy. A religious reign over hearts was distinguished from a legal rule over bodies. Free and willing faith and untamed and independent understanding were found to be the essential characteristics of a religious society and the outward ritual aspects were recognized as secondary effects of the above. In none of these discussions were the boundaries of the domain of extrareligious discourse violated. Religious jurists and exegetes were never invited to enter the arena of theological and religious debate. The question of religion was deemed too important to be trusted to uncritical legal exegeses cut off from autonomous rational principles.

From Chapter 8 of *Reason Freedom, and Democracy in Islam: Essential Writings of Abdolkarim Soroush*. Edited by Mahmoud Sadri and Ahmad Sadri, © 2000. By Permission of Oxford University Press, Inc.

The role of rationality in the arena of religion has, thus far, been that of a timid and discreet servant of understanding and defense of religion. However, defense and affirmation cannot be complete without critique and analysis. The enterprise of rationality is an all-or-nothing project. One may not employ reason to attest to the truth of one's opinions, without leaving the door open to its fault-finding critique. The attempt to enjoy the sweet affirmation of reason without tasting its bitter reproach is pure self delusion. Writing books in defense of women's rights, human rights, and the system of government in Islam, summoning reason to affirm and defend the truth of one's arguments, while turning a deaf ear to rational critique of the rest of one's beliefs exemplifies a half-finished enterprise that falls far short of the requirements of reasoned discourse and the standards of rationality.

Invitation to religious democracy is an invitation to the thoroughgoing project of religious rationality, a rationality that contains gains along with losses. It is an invitation to a determined methodology with undetermined results, an invitation to examined versus emulated religiosity. It is true that in religious societies imitation prevails, appearance takes primacy over essence, and the apologetic reason rises above the critical reason. However, these mind-numbing emulations and thought-killing rigidities have always been decried and condemned by the anguished and the vigilant. The invitation to religious democracy is an invitation to the realization of the freedom of faith, respect for dynamic understanding, and the establishment of a system that fosters and invigorates such ideals.

In democratic societies, the path of examined religiosity is more open and inviting. Those who appreciate the value and sanctity of religion and the glory of investigation will never doubt that a single examined faith is nobler than a thousand imitated, shaky, and weak beliefs. "The religious despotism," a term perceptively coined by the knowledgeable juris-consult, logician, and theologian of the last century. Ayatollah Na'ini, is indeed insurmountable except by the help of such a rational democracy. Religious despotism is most intransigent because a religious despot views his rule not only his right but his duty. Only a religious democracy that secures and shelters faith can be secure and sheltered from such self-righteous and antireligious rule.

Discussison Questions for II - C

1. In The World House, published in 1967, Martin Luther King Jr. recognizes that "All men are interdependent. . . . The agony of the poor impoverishes the rich; the betterment of the poor enriches the rich. We are inevitably our brother's keeper because we are our brother's brother." How do religion and democracy merge into one another for King?

2. Father Drinan asks, "Will there ever be an age when God and Caesar can coexist in peace? Law is a feeble instrument to bring about that laudable objective. If law is to be effective, it must be joined with love—and love for others is at the core of every religion and every code of conduct." Still, he believes that the influence of international declarations gives people greater incentives to live by the Golden Rule. Is that evident in our time?

3. According to the Dalai Lama, "Like Buddhism, modern democracy is based on the principle that all human beings are essentially equal, and that each of us has an equal right to life, liberty, and happiness. . . . Thus not only are Buddhism and democracy compatible, they are rooted in a common understanding of equality and potential of every individual." Do any other religions have as much in common with democracy—at their very roots—as Buddhism? Discuss.

4. Why are there limits to our individual freedom in a democracy, and what are they?

5. Jonathan Sacks sees "fundamentalism, like imperialism . . . [as] the attempt to impose a single truth on a plural world. It is the Tower of Babel of our time." What does he propose as a new paradigm that goes beyond pluralism? What are the limitations of pluralism, in his view? What are the strengths of "the dignity of difference?"

6. Irving Greenberg claims that even God is self-limiting and that human beings—in a democratic context—must also be self-limiting. Explain why democracy requires limits and pluralism—and why pluralism does not force one to give up his/her own faith?

7. How does Arkoun's perspective on human rights differ from or agree with views of other thinkers on the relationship between religion and democracy?

II - D

The Radical Sanity
of the Pluralist Paradigm

The writers in this section talk the talk and walk the walk of what can be seen as "the radical sanity of the pluralist paradigm." For them, from their various perspectives, pluralism is, in our imperfect world, the best or only principle on which to base our attitudes and actions. Martha Nussbaum and Cornel West see the essential role that poetry and music play in creating the pluralist reality, and Bishop Tutu rejoices in the wonder of the end of apartheid in South Africa as an example of "anything can happen" in the world, in this time. They at once detect and help to create a "beat," a rhythmic progress from long held hatreds and fears toward a pluralistic, harmonious global community.

Introduction to a New America

Diana L. Eck

. . . We must be clear about the fact that . . . diversity alone does not constitute pluralism. It is plain evidence of the new religious America but whether we are able to work together across the lines of religious difference to create a society in which we actually know one another remains to be seen. On New Hampshire Avenue, that process is just beginning. Schoolchildren come for visits to the mosque and the Cambodian temple; the two churches that flank the Islamic center lend their parking lots for the two large Eid prayers; and all these communities have a growing awareness of the InterFaith Conference of Metropolitan Washington.

Beyond the changing landscape of our cities, the Pluralism Project is interested in how these religious traditions are changing as they take root in American soil. When Tristan, one of our summer researchers, interviewed a Vietnamese monk in Phoenix, the monk said, "We have to take the plant of Buddhism out of its Asian pot and plant it in the soil of Arizona." The monk's observation could apply to any of the new religious communities. What does Buddhism look like as it begins to grow in its new soil? What will Islam become as it spreads into the suburban life of Houston? What will Hinduism look like as it takes root in central Minneapolis, where Hindu young people take ski trips together and celebrate their high school graduation at the temple with a *puja*? Religions are not like stones passed from hand to hand through the ages. They are dynamic movements, more like rivers—flowing, raging, creative, splitting, converging. The history of religions is unfolding before our eyes. Perhaps nowhere in the world is it more interesting to study the process of dynamic religious change in this new century than in America.

Not only is America changing these religions, but these religions are also changing America. This too is an important question for ongoing study. What does this new religious diversity mean for American electoral politics, for the continuing interpretation of church-state issues by the Supreme Court? What does it mean for American public education and the controversies of school boards? What will it mean for colleges and universities with an increasingly multireligious student body? What about hospitals and health care programs with an increasingly diverse patient population? While many people are just beginning to become aware of the changing religious landscape, the issues it has begun to raise for the American pluralist experiment are already on the agenda of virtually every public institution.

Our new questions are not only civic, however, but also spiritual and theological. How will Christians and Jews, long dominant in America, respond to this new diversity? Churches, synagogues, and theological schools have barely begun to take notice of this new religious reality. Yet with the changing landscape, the entire context of ministry has begun to change. Adherents of other faiths are no longer distant metaphorical neighbors in some other part of the world but next-door neighbors. A block down the street from a United Church of Christ congregation in Garden Grove, California, is the Lien Hoa Buddhist temple, the home of several Vietnamese Buddhist monks. Next door to the Atonement Lutheran Church in San Diego is San Diego's largest Islamic Center. In Flushing, New York, a synagogue stands next door to a storefront Sikh gurdwara, across the street from Swaminarayan Hindu temple, and down the street from the Ganesha Hindu Temple. And yet few theological schools are able to equip Christian or Jewish clergy for their changing educational roles in this new ministerial context. The issue of living in a pluralist society and thinking theologically about the questions it poses is important today for every community of faith. How do we think about our own faith as we come into deeper relationship with people of other faiths and as we gain a clearer understanding of their religious lives?

As a Christian, a Montana-born, lifelong Methodist who has lived and studied in India, I too have asked this question. How do I articulate my faith in a world in which neighbors, colleagues, and students live deeply religious lives in other communities of faith? When I began my studies of the Hindu tradition, living in the sacred city of Banaras, I tried to articulate, in *Banaras, City of Light*, what this holy city and all it represents means for Hindus. Further along life's journey, I wrote *Encountering God: A Spiritual Tradition from Boseman to Banaras*, which tackled another equally difficult question: What does Banaras and all it represents mean for me, as a Christian? Through the years I have found my own faith not threatened, but broadened and deepened by the study of Hindu, Buddhist, Muslim, and Sikh traditions of faith. And I have found that only as a Christian pluralist could I be faithful to the mystery and the presence of the one I call God. Being a Christian pluralist means daring to encounter people of very different faith traditions and defining my faith not by its borders, but by its roots.

Many Christians would not agree with me. In the fall of 1999 the Southern Baptist Convention published a prayer guide to enable Christians to pray for Hindus during Diwali, their fall festival of lights. It spoke of the 900 million Hindus who are "lost in the hopeless darkness of Hinduism . . . who worship gods which are not God." Many Christians have no trouble at all speaking of "our God" in exclusivist terms as if God had no dealings with Hindus. The problem with such a response, however, is that it misunderstands both Hindu worship and Hindu experience of God. The American Hindus who carried placards protesting the Southern Baptist prayer guide before the Second Baptist Church in Houston did so not because they were averse to being the focus of Christian prayers, but because the characterization of their religious tradition was so ill-informed and ignorant. As I would put it in the language of my own tradition, it is fine for Baptists to bear witness to their faith; indeed, it is incumbent upon Christians to do so. But it is not fine for us to bear false witness against neighbors of other faiths.

Articulating one's own faith anew in a world of many faiths is a task for people of every religious tradition today, and in every tradition there are thinkers and movements taking up this task. We cannot live in a world in which our economies and markets are global, our political awareness is global, our business relationships take us to every continent, and the Internet connects us with colleagues half a world away and yet live in Friday, Saturday, or Sunday with the ideas of God that are essentially provincial, imagining that somehow the one we call God has been primarily concerned with us and our tribe. No one would dream of operating in the business or political world with ideas about Russia, India, or China that were formed fifty, a hundred, or five hundred years ago. I might sing, "Give me that old-time religion! It's good enough for me!" with as much gusto as anyone, but in my heart I know that the old-time religion is not "good enough" unless those of us who claim it are able to grapple honestly and faithfully with the new questions, challenges, and knowledge posted to us by the vibrant world of many living faiths. To be good enough, the old-time religion has to be up to the challenges of an intricately interdependent world.

Theological questions and civic questions are different, however. And it is important that we understand the difference. No matter how we evaluate religions that are different from our own, no matter how we think about religion if we are atheists or secularists, the covenants of citizenship to which we adhere place us on common ground. The Southern Baptists who pray for Hindus who are "lost" are perfectly free to do so. Their theological ideas are not governed by our Constitution, but their commitment to the free exercise of religion, even for Hindus, is. For a moment in September of 2000, the conservative Family Research Council became confused about this distinction. When the first-ever Hindu invocation was given at the U.S. House of Representatives, the council denounced it as a move toward "ethical chaos," saying it was "one more indication that our nation is drifting from its Judeo-Christian roots. . . ." On second thought, the council issued a much-needed clarification: "We affirm the truth of Christianity, but it is not our position that America's Constitution forbids representatives of religions other than Christianity from praying before Congress."

Today all of us are challenged to claim for a new age the very principles of religious freedom that shaped our nation. We must find ways to articulate them anew, whether we are Christian, Jewish, Muslim, Buddhist, or secular Americans. We must embrace the religious diversity that comes with our commitment to religious freedom, and as we move into the new millennium we must find ways to make the differences that have divided people the world over the very source of our strength here in the U.S. It will require moving beyond laissez-faire inattention to religion to a vigorous attempt to understand the religions of our neighbors. And it will require the engagement of our religious traditions in the common tasks of our civil society. Today, right here in the U.S., we have an opportunity to create a vibrant and hopeful pluralism, in a world of increasing fragmentation where there are few models for a truly pluralistic, multi-religious society.

Radical Evil in the Lockean State: The Neglect of the Political Emotions

Martha C. Nussbaum

How can a respectful pluralistic society shore up the fragile bases of toleration, especially in a world in which we need to cultivate toleration not only within each state, but also between peoples in this interlocking world?

Kant was surely right in thinking that one very important part of the solution is the vigilant protection of freedoms of speech, press, and scholarship. Intolerance thrives in a situation in which opinion is curtailed, and we may observe that intolerant groups usually if not always seek the curtailment of these freedoms as a road to domination. Consider the situation of the Hindu right in India today. These groups want, in essence, to turn a pluralistic respectful Lockean state into a non-respectful Hindu-first society in which norms of ethnic purity are used to establish who is a first-class and who a second-class citizen. Central to their operations are attacks on academic freedom, the freedom of scholars to publish dissident views (of history, of religion, of politics), and the freedom of opinion generally. It seems just right in this case for the proponents of pluralism and toleration to focus on shoring up the Kantian freedoms, as an essential bulwark of the other political liberties. But this case shows, as well, that a possibly fatal threat to the very existence of a Lockean democracy can arise and become strong even though the Kantian freedoms have been, until now anyway, pretty well protected. So what more might be done, along Rousseauian lines without his illiberal strategies?

One thing that a society may certainly do, and that most societies do already, is to attach rituals and ceremonies to the basic freedoms protected by the society, inspiring citizens to love those values by linking the values to music, art, and ritual. This strategem is dangerous, given the propensity of all forms of patriotism to lead to demonization of foreigners and local "subversives." We see in the case of the Hindu right in India how such patriotic values can be hijacked and turned to the services of radical evil. Nonetheless, it seems to me that there are reasonable ways to institutionalize such ceremonies that do not buy into these dangers. Where toleration is concerned, a reasonable "civil religion" would include, for example, a celebration of the diversity of traditions and comprehensive doctrines that are contained within a nation, as a source of its strength and richness. In general, there is much that the tolerant state may do by way of persuasion and rhetorical undergirding, without infringing on the freedoms of speech, assembly, and publication of those who think differently.

An attractive further proposal was made by John Stuart Mill in his essay on "The Utility of Religion."[1] Here Mill, recognizing the importance of religious sentiments in giving force to moral motivation, suggests what (following August Comte and others) he calls a "The Religion of Humanity," a moral ideal that could be promulgated through public education.[2] According to this moral ideal, a good person is one who cares deeply about humanity generally. Her thoughts and feelings learn the habit of being carried away from her own parochial concerns; they are habitually fixed on this "unselfish object, loved and pursued as an end for its own sake." She learns to view helping others as a part of her own good: she identifies her good with that of humanity as a whole, and thinks of her afterlife as the life of those who follow her. She learns, in these ways and others, that helping others is not a sacrifice, but an intrinsic good. Thus she learns a "morality grounded on large and wise views of the good of the whole, neither sacrificing the individual to the aggregate nor the aggregate to the individual, but giving to duty on the one hand and to freedom and spontaneity on the other their proper province" (108).

To the imagined objection that human beings cannot really learn to be motivated by universal concerns, Mill responds with some very insightful remarks about patriotism and its force:

> When we consider how ardent a sentiment in favourable circumstances of education, the love of country has become, we cannot judge it impossible that the love of that larger country, the world, may be nursed into similar strength, both as a source of elevated emotion and as a principle of duty.[3]

These ideas are closely linked to some that I have tried to develop, in *Upheavals of Thought,* concerning compassion as a moral sentiment that can be cultivated by public institutions and public education. I have argued that a liberal society, without offending against respect for pluralism, can still employ a moral ideal of this sort, and promote a moral education aimed at underwriting it. This ideal would serve as a basis for public political culture, in connection with public norms of equality and respect. In effect, such a moral education would be the psychological underpinning to public norms that can command a Rawlsian "overlapping consensus", and thus, as I argue, it need not be seen as divisive or illiberal, when made part of a public education.

How, more precisely, would this moral education be institutionalized? A good part of it, I argue, would in fact take the form of developing institutions that express the views of equal respect and due attention to the needs of all: a just tax system, a just health care system, a just welfare system. But institutions remain stable only when human beings have the will to sustain them, a fact that the collapse of social democracy in the United States, since the Reagan era, has made an all too vivid reality. Therefore, I argue, public education at all levels (and private education too), should focus on putting forward something like Mill's religion of humanity, conveying the sense that all human lives are of equal worth, and all worthy of being lived with dignity and a decent minimum level of well-being.

More concretely, public education can cultivate awareness of the problems human beings face on the way to their well-being, in different parts of one's own nation and in different parts of the world, and can impart a sense of urgency concerning the importance of giving all world citizens decent life chances. Children can learn with increasing sophistication the economic and political obstacles human beings face on the way to their well-being, and can learn to see ways in which a just society might overcome these problems. At the same time, education can try to minimize the role of greed and competitive accumulation in society, by portraying greedy accumulation in a negative light and showing how it subverts the legitimate strivings of others—a teaching to which the major religious and secular comprehensive doctrines certainly give lip service, even if they do not always insist on it in practice.

Where toleration is concerned, the "religion of humanity" takes, in the first instance, an institutional form, in the form of strong protections for religious liberty and a support for the idea of equal respect for comprehensive doctrines. (A doctrine of non-establishment is one very usual and valuable means of promoting equal respect.) Enhanced penalties for crimes involving ethnic, racial, and religious hatred would also be prominent parts of the institutional side of such a program, expressing society's very strong disapproval of intolerance and the actions to which it can give rise.

Walt Whitman understood, and repeatedly asserted, that the civic fabric of a democracy cannot be held together by laws and institutions alone: "To hold men together by paper and seal or by compulsion is no account" (Blue Ontario's Shore 130). What is needed is something which aggregates all in a living principle" (131)—and that, he insists, can be supplied only by poets. Writing during the Civil War, he says that the U.S. needs poets more than any other country does; "Their Presidents shall not be their common referee so much as their poets shall" (133).

Why are poets needed? This is a large topic, but the connection of poetry with the emotions is a central part of it. An insistent theme in Whitman's poetry is the relationship we have to minorities in our society: African-Americans, women, and homosexuals. Whitman understood that laws can say that all citizens are equal, but only poetry can construct sentiments that lead all citizens to acknowledge that equality, because only poetry can characterize the suffering of exclusion in a way that moves us to put an end to it, and only poetry can characterize what we stigmatize and hate in ways that make us see it differently. Crucial to this project is forging a new idea of the body. My own very Whitmanesque view about the nature of "radical evil" is that a certain shame and disgust at our very humanity leads, under many social circumstances, to the stigmatization of others. Whitman saw his task, therefore, as creating a new relationship to the body, one of love and delight rather than shame and disgust. Like Tagore, Whitman understood that emotions supportive of respect for all the different citizens of a great nation, whatever their race, gender, or religion, required working vigilantly against the tendency to stigmatize the different by portraying people or groups as disgusting, as bearers of some type of bodily contamination or dirtiness. This human tendency, which I call projective disgust, is a flight from something in ourselves; it therefore can be countered only by a reconstructed relation to ourselves and our bodily fluids, which Whitman again and again tries to forge—above all in "I Sing the Body Electric," but throughout "Song of Myself" and many shorter poems as well.

Whitman's poetry, like Mill's religion of humanity, contains ideas of transcendence. First of all, it contains the idea of what I have called "internal transcendence," the transcendence of racism and other forms of oppression in justice, the transcendence of the Civil

War in the form of a restored and aspiringly just nation, the transcendence of the hatred of difference in the form of an image of New York, which represents for Whitman the idea that people different and unsettling to one another might live in peace, and chaotic turbulent amity, with one another. Second, it also contains a Millean idea of the continuity of all lives, the way in which the lives of soldiers dead in the war survive in the blades of grass upon their tomb, the way in which all of us survive in our fellow world citizens and the progress of humanity. It repudiates as harmful not the bare desire for transcendence, but rather a disgust at one's human body, which is seen by Whitman to be strongly linked with the repudiation of particular groups and people. (To his list, we should add the repudiation of people with bodily and mental disabilities, who are all too often shunned because of an anxiety they evoke in the people who would like to think their bodies free from flaw.)

Public poetry is likely to be unsettling, as Whitman's poems have always been found unsettling. And yet the sheer richness of language and image in them leads the reader in, until the difficult and challenging images prove acceptable—even images of the relationship between self and soul as one of homoerotic intercourse, images of women being freed to bathe and dance with naked men, images of black men eating with white men and even exchanging clothing with them. When one considers the extraordinary fact that a poet who frankly challenged all the sources of disgust and stigma in American society is beloved and is taught to every school child in the country, one can see the magnitude of the task that Whitman has accomplished.

It is hardly necessary to mention the fact that high minded philosophical sentiments compatible with this hope [of tolerance], if written as you or I would write them, or even as John Stuart Mill would have written them, could not on their own have moved large masses of people to support its cause. Martin Luther King's poetic and rhetorical genius played a key role in getting people to support the non-violent movement, and in getting still other people to understand what it was all about. In this way, rhetoric and emotion changed history. If King hadn't been this sort of poet, we can hardly say what would have happened next. King, to my mind, advances civil religion in the best sense. In its Gandhian vision of non-violence and its reliance on the tradition of Constitutional rights, it is a civil religion in a way that is compatible with the vision of Locke and Kant; it does not rely on Rousseauian coercion. Moreover, although the speech relies for some of its effects on familiarity with Judaeo-Christian prophetic texts, it uses those texts in a non-sectarian way, as it also uses Shakespeare and "America the Beautiful." Its sentiments, and its images too, can be endorsed by people who do not belong to that religious tradition, and also by people who do not have any religion.

Endnotes

[1] "Utility of Religion," in Mill, *Three Essays on Religion*, (New York: Prometheus Book, 1998), 70–122.

[2] For a discussion of the essay and the influence of Comtean ideas in nineteenth century English philosophy, generally I am indebted to a fine unpublished paper by Daniel Brudney.

[3] P. 107.

Exodus and Revolution

Michael Walzer

Compared with political messianism, Exodus makes for a cautious and moderate politics. Compared with "the old type of social struggle" or with the even more common passivity and acquiescence of the oppressed, it makes for a revolutionary politics. But these terms are misleading. As we have seen, the Exodus story is open to interpretation, and one can imagine social democrats and (some) Bolsheviks at home within it. The biblical text tells a tale of argument and contention, and the commentators read the text in the same spirit; there is always "another interpretation." Political messianism is quite different. One can calculate endlessly the number of days until the Last Days; there is always another calculation; but once a decision has been made to force the End, there is no room for argument. Then politics is absolute, enemies satanic, compromise impossible. Exodus politics slides, sometimes, toward absolutism—as in a sermon preached by the Puritan minister Stephen Marshall to the House of Commons in 1641: "All people are cursed or blessed according as they do or do not join their strength and give their best assistance to the Lord's people against their enemies." The curses and blessing derive, I suppose, from Deuteronomy, but Marshall comes close to the later Bolshevik slogan, "You are either for us or against us." It's only when the struggle is an ultimate one that choice can be so radically restricted. For men and women working within the Exodus tradition, however, choice more commonly takes on a different character. There is no ultimate struggle, but a long series of decisions, backslidings, and reforms. The apocalyptic war between "the Lord's people" and "their enemies" can't readily be located within Exodus.

Absolutism is effectively barred, I think, by the very character of the people, frightened, stubborn, contentious, and at the same time, members of the covenant. The people can't be killed (not all of them anyway)

From *Exodus and Revolution* by Michael Walzer, pp. 146–149. Copyright © 1985 by Basic Books. Reprinted by permission of BASIC BOOKS, a member of Perseus Books, L.L.C.

or cast aside or miraculously transformed. They must be led, chastised, defended, argued with, educated—activities that undercut and defeat any simple designation of "enemies." The revolutionary idea of a holy nation does breed enemies, of course, but the struggle is never so melodramatic as Marshall's formula suggests. The presence of the people makes for realism, not only because some among the people are tough-minded and skeptical realists, asking hard questions, like the psalmist's "Can God furnish a table in the wilderness?" or the midrashic rabbi's "on what grounds do you slay three thousand men in one day?" The people also make for realism because the pace of the march must be set with their feelings in mind, because their rebellions must be dealt with, leaders chosen from their midst, and the law expounded in their hearing. They can't easily be divided into friends and enemies; their very stiff-neckedness is somehow admirable. Many of them still retained an affection for Egypt, wrote Benjamin Franklin in a "Comparison of the Conduct of the Ancient Jews and of the Anti-Federalists," but "on the whole it appears [from the text] that the Israelites were a people jealous of their newly acquired liberty." They were only inexperienced and, like the Americans, "worked upon by artful men. . . ."

This is a typical piece of Exodus politics, but it doesn't quite suggest the sobering power of the biblical story, for Franklin was hardly disposed to think of the Anti-Federalists as the representatives of Anti-Christ. In the writings of contemporary liberation theologians, the power of the story is more evident. One can feel in their books and essays a constant thrust toward political messianism, but since Exodus is the standard reference for liberation, and the promised land the standard goal, there is also a strong sense of this-worldly complexity. Exodus history and politics work as a constraint on Christian eschatology. Liberation is not a movement from our fallen state to the messianic kingdom but from "the slavery, exploitation, and alienation of Egypt" to a land where the people can live "with human dignity." The movement takes place in historical time; it is the hard and continuous work of men and women. The best of the liberation theologians explicitly warns his readers against "absolutizing [the] revolution" and falling into idolatry toward "unavoidably ambiguous human achievements." This, again, is Exodus politics.

So pharaonic oppression, deliverance, Sinai, and Canaan are still with us, powerful memories shaping our perceptions of the political world. The "door of hope" is still open; things are not what they might be—even when what they might be isn't totally different from what they are. This is a central theme in Western thought, always present though elaborated in many different ways. We still believe, or many of us do, what the Exodus first taught, or what it has commonly been taken to teach, about the meaning and possibility of politics and about its proper form:

- first, that wherever you live, it is probably Egypt;
- second, that there is a better place, a world more attractive, a promised land;
- and third, that "the way to the land is through the wilderness." There is no way to get from here to there except by joining together and marching.

Putting on Our Democratic Armor

Cornel West

Despite the Constantinian captivity of much of the Christian movement here and abroad, the prophetic tradition has a deep legacy of
providing extraordinary strength of commitment and vision that helps
us to care in a palpable way about the injustices we see around us. In
our own time this was the fire that drove Martin Luther King Jr.,
Rabbi Abraham Joshua Heschel, Dorothy Day, and millions of other
Americans to deepen our democratic project. This prophetic tradition
is an infectious and invigorating way of life and struggle. It generates
the courage to care and act in light of a universal moral vision that
indicts the pervasive corruption, greed, and bigotry in our souls and
society. It awakens us from the fashionable ways of being indifferent
to other people's suffering or from subtle ways of remaining numb to
the social misery in our midst. Prophetic love of justice unleashes ethical energy and political engagement that explodes all forms of our
egocentric predicaments or tribalistic mind-sets. Its telling signs are
ethical witness (including maybe martyrdom for some), moral consis-
tency, and political activism—all crucial elements of our democratic
armor for the fight against corrupt elite power.

Yet in our postmodern world of pervasive consumerism and hedo-
nism, narcissism and cynicism, skepticism and nihilism, the Socratic
love of wisdom and prophetic love of justice may appear hopeless.
Who has not felt overwhelmed by dread and despair when confronting the atrocities and barbarities of our world? And surely
a cheap optimism or trite sentimentalism will not sustain us. We need
a bloodstained Socratic love and tear-soaked prophetic love fueled
by a hard-won tragicomic hope. Our democratic fight against corrupt
elite power needs the vital strength provided by the black American
invention of the blues. The blues is the most profound interpretation
of tragicomic hope in America. The blues encourages us to confront
the harsh realities of our personal and political lives unflinchingly

without innocent sentimentalism or coldhearted cynicism. The blues forges a mature hope that fortifies us on the slippery tightrope of Socratic questioning and prophetic witness in imperial America.

This black American interpretation of tragicomic hope is rooted in a love of freedom. It proceeds from a free inquisitive spirit that highlights imperial America's weak will to racial justice. It is a sad yet sweet indictment of abusive power and blind greed run amok. It is a melancholic yet melioristic stance toward America's denial of its terrors and horrors heaped on others. It yields a courage to hope for betterment against the odds without a sense of revenge or resentment. It revels in a dark joy of freely thinking, acting, and loving under severe constraints of unfreedom.

I have always marveled at how such an unfree people as blacks in America created the freest forms in America, such as blues and jazz. I have often pondered how we victims of American democracy invented such odes to democratic individuality and community as in the blues and jazz. And . . . I now wonder whether American democracy can survive without learning from the often-untapped democratic energies and lessons of black Americans. How does one affirm a life of mature autonomy while recognizing that evil is inseparable from freedom? How does one remain open and ready for meaningful solidarity with the very people who hate you? Frederick Douglass and Bessie Smith, Ida B. Wells-Barnett and Duke Ellington, Sarah Vaughan and Martin Luther King Jr., Ella Baker and Louis Armstrong all are wise voices in a deep democratic tradition in America that may provide some clue to these crucial questions in our time. They all knew that even if the tears of the world are a constant quantity and that the air is full of our cries, we can and should still embark on a democratic quest for wisdom, justice, and freedom.

This kind of tragicomic hope is dangerous—and potentially subversive—because it can never be extinguished. Like laughter, dance, and music, it is a form of elemental freedom that cannot be eliminated or snuffed out by any elite power. Instead, it is inexorably resilient and inescapably seductive–even contagious. It is wedded to a long and rich tradition of humanist pursuits of wisdom, justice, and freedom from Amos through Socrates to Ellison. The high modern moments in this tradition–Shakespeare, Beethoven, Chekhov, Coltrane—enact and embody a creative weaving of the Socratic, prophetic, and tragicomic elements into profound interpretations of what it means to be human. These three elements constitute the most sturdy democratic armor available to us in our fight against corrupt elite power. They represent the best of what has been bequeathed to us and what we look like when we are at our best—as deep democrats and as human beings.

This democratic armor allows us to absorb any imperial and xenophobic blows that still persist. It permits us to face any anti-democratic foe and persevere. It encourages us to fight any form of dogma or nihilism and still endure. It only requires that we be true to ourselves by choosing to be certain kinds of human beings and democratic citizens indebted to a deep democratic tradition and committed to keeping it vital and vibrant. This democratic vocation wedded to an unstoppable predilection for possibility may not guarantee victory, but it does enhance the probability of hard-won progress. And if we lose our precious democratic experiment, let it be said that we went down swinging like Ella Fitzgerald and Muhammad Ali—with style, grace, and a smile that signifies that the seeds of democracy matters will flower and flourish somewhere and somehow and remember our gallant efforts.

Islam and the Challenge of Democracy

Khaled Abou El Fadl

Much of the Islamic discourse is captive to the historical experience of colonialism as well as the reality of contemporary imperialism, and so it is held hostage to a traumatized condition in which there is an intense concern for autonomy and liberation; but it is also coupled with an oblivious disregard of the need for self-definition. In many ways, the problem is that confronted with the often gruesome political realities of the Muslim world, one is seriously tempted to surrender to a deep sense of cynicism about the claims of democracy, freedom, and dignity for all. But the abusive use of moral universals to justify immoral conduct ought not dissuade anyone from recognizing the worthiness and desirability of a political system that tends to limit the abusive use of power and augments the protections afforded to individuals so that they can discharge their obligations as God's vicegerents without being at the mercy of despots.

I believe that if democracy is to become a systematic normative goal of large numbers of Muslims in Muslim countries, it will have to be anchored in both Islam and modernity. To achieve this objective, a serious discourse that negotiates between, but does not dismiss, the past and the present and that negotiates between slavish imitation and unprincipled and self-indulgent inventiveness is imperative. This is exactly what makes the engagements between my interlocutors and me particularly valuable. The fact that this civil debate is taking place while the coercion and oppressiveness of terrorism, invasions, and war are galvanizing the attention of the world only serves to emphasize the crucial need for a greater respect for human rights and the democratic practice of civil discourse.

No Future Without Forgiveness

Desmond Tutu

It is crucial . . . that we keep remembering that negotiations, peace talks, forgiveness, and reconciliation happen most frequently not between friends, not between those who like one another. They happen precisely because people are at loggerheads and detest one another as only enemies can. But enemies are potential allies, friends, colleagues, and collaborators. This is not just utopian idealism. The first democratically-elected government of South Africa was a government of National Unity made up of members of political parties that were engaged in a life-and-death struggle. The man who headed it had been incarcerated for twenty-seven years as a dangerous terrorist. If it could happen there, surely it can happen in other places. Perhaps God chose such an unlikely place deliberately to show the world that it can be done anywhere.

If the protagonists in the world's conflicts began to make symbolic gestures for peace, changed the way they described their enemies, and began talking to them, their actions might change too. For instance, what is it doing for future relations in the Middle East to go on constructing Jewish settlements in what is accepted to be Palestinian territory when this causes so much bitterness and resentment among the Palestinians, who feel belittled and abused? What legacy does it leave for the children of those who are destined to be neighbors? I have asked similar questions when Arab nations have seemed so completely unrealistic in thinking they could destroy Israel. What a wonderful gift to the world, especially as we enter a new millennium, if true peace would come in the land of those who say *salama*, or *shalom*, in the land of the Prince of Peace.

Peace is possible, especially if today's adversaries were to imagine themselves becoming friends and begin acting in ways that would promote such a friendship developing in reality. It would be wonderful if, as they negotiated, they tried to find ways of accommodating each other's needs. A readiness to make concessions is a sign of strength, not weakness. And it can be worthwhile sometimes to lose a battle in order in the end to win the war. Those who are engaged in negotiations for peace and prosperity are striving after such a splendid, such a priceless goal that it should be easier to find ways for all to be winners than to fight; for negotiators to make it a point that no one loses face, that no one emerges empty handed, with nothing to place before his or her constituency. How one wishes that negotiators would avoid having bottom lines and too many preconditions. In negotiations we are, as in the process of forgiveness, seeking to give all the chance to begin again. The rigid will have a tough time. The flexible, those who are ready to make principled compromises, end up being the victors.

I have said ours was a flawed commission. Despite that, I do want to assert as eloquently and as passionately as I can that it was, in an imperfect world, the best possible instrument so far devised to deal with the kind of situation that confronted us after democracy was established in our motherland. With all its imperfections, what we have tried to do in South Africa has attracted the attention of the world. This tired, disillusioned, cynical world, hurting so frequently and so grievously, has marveled at a process that holds out considerable hope in the midst of much that negates hope. People in the different places that I have visited and where I have spoken about the Truth and Reconciliation process see in the flawed attempt a beacon of hope, a possible paradigm for dealing with situations where violence, conflict, turmoil, and sectional strife have seemed endemic, conflicts that mostly take place not between warring nations but within the same nation. At the end of their conflicts, the warring groups in Northern Ireland, the Balkans, the Middle East, Sri Lanka, Burma, Afghanistan, Angola, the Sudan, the two Congos, and elsewhere are going to have to sit down together to determine just how they will be able to live together amicably, how they might have a shared future devoid of strife, given the bloody past that they have recently lived through. They see more than just a glimmer of hope in what we have attempted in South Africa.

God does have a sense of humor. Who in their right minds could ever have imagined South Africa to be an example of anything but the most ghastly awfulness, of how not to order a nation's race relations and its governance? We South Africans were the unlikeliest lot and that is precisely why God has chosen us. We cannot really claim much credit ourselves for what we have achieved. We were destined for perdition and were plucked out of total annihilation. We were a hopeless case if there ever was one. God intends that others might look at us and take courage. God wants to point to us as a possible beacon of hope, a possible paradigm, and to say, "Look at South Africa. They had a nightmare called apartheid. It has ended. Northern Ireland (or wherever), your nightmare will end too. They had a problem regarded as intractable. They are resolving it. No problem anywhere can ever again be considered to be intractable. There is hope for you too."

Our experiment is going to succeed because God wants us to succeed, not for our glory and aggrandizement but for the sake of God's world. God wants to show that there is life after conflict and repression—that because of forgiveness there is a future.

Foundering?

Noah Feldman

Even if the Iraqis manage to ratify a constitution, it is bound to dodge and defer many big questions. Just look at ours.

When a constitution succeeds, its framers come to be regarded as visionaries. They are seen in retrospect to have predicted future difficulties and dealt with them ingeniously, by building a machine that would run of itself. From the inside, though, constitution drafting is not so philosophical and frictionless; it does not take place under the aspect of the eternal. The immediate politics of the moment dominate, along with the lurking fear that if the constitution is not ratified, national collapse may follow.

In Baghdad today, as in Philadelphia in 1787, constitution writing means horse-trading, improvisation, dispute and deferral. As Iraq's constitutional process nears its first deadline—a draft text is supposed to be approved by the interim parliament by August 15—the members of the constitutional committee are certainly feeling the heat. They are busily bargaining with one another, staging walkouts and issuing ultimatums, and gambling that the public will embrace their new design for a unified state. All the while, they are trying to avoid the fate of their colleagues who have been assassinated.

Under these tense circumstances, deferral is understandably the order of the day. The less the constitution says about controversial issues, the greater the likelihood that it will be ratified. Even in peaceful Philadelphia, after all, the framers kept the word "slavery" out of the Constitution, preferring euphemistic denial, as in the provision stating that "the Migration or Importation of such Persons as any of the States now existing shall think proper to admit, shall not be prohibited by Congress prior to the Year one thousand eight hundred and eight." Guaranteeing the slave trade for 20 years was a classic instance of the constitutional punt. Such dubious compromises bought the United States more than 70 years, even if they ultimately failed to avert civil war.

For the Iraqis, the elephant in the room is the relationship between government and religion: can Iraq be a democracy and an Islamic state at the same time? When I worked as an adviser to the Iraqis who drafted last year's interim constitution, this fraught question occupied the authors until almost the last minute. Leaked portions of the new constitution, still open to debate and revision, show that the matter remains as tricky as ever. Equality for all citizens is guaranteed, but Islamic law is also prescribed for marriage, divorce and inheritance. Of course, some elements of Islamic family law might mandate gender inequality; to address that possibility, one draft reportedly provides that religion would trump equality if the two conflict.

These tentative efforts to reconcile Islam and democratic equality ensure that future Iraqi legislators and jurists will have to figure out just what it means to treat Islam as "a source of law" or, perhaps, "a main source." At this time, it is simply not possible to work out Iraq's religious identity without alienating either clerics or secular rights organizations.

Meanwhile, the specter of a national breakup bedevils the Iraqi negotiators, just as it did the drafters in Philadelphia. Kurdish autonomy, politely relabeled "federalism," may be the greatest stumbling block to reaching a constitutional deal. Many Arab Iraqis will experience an initial shock when they look closely at the de facto self-government that the Kurds have negotiated for themselves. Meanwhile, ownership of disputed Kirkuk and its oil fields cannot be assigned without calling ratification into doubt. As in the U.S. Constitution, "secession" itself will go unmentioned—allowing politicians to claim in the future that the omission either allows or prohibits Kurdistan from establishing itself on its own.

But the bottom line is that Arab Iraqis, like Northerners who objected to slavery but cared more for Union, have no choice but to acquiesce in vague language that opens the door to Kurdish demands. The Kurds have a substantial military force and a strong friendship with the U.S.; who is going to take their self-government away from them? Anyway, federalism always entails tension between a central government and states' rights. So Iraqis must gamble that their precarious arrangements do not lead to secession and civil slaughter.

A constitution that acclimates a people to living with contradiction pretty much guarantees unintended consequences. The Philadelphia framers decided to leave out a bill of rights, since they worried that listing some rights might imply the nonexistence of others. But when the states' ratifying conventions insisted on specific guarantees, the first Congress went to work. Today the 10 amendments (originally plotted as 12, with our First as the less impressive Third) seem more like universal principles than a political afterthought.

For the Iraqis, the unexpected results lie in the not-too-distant future. But to get there, to arrive in a world where courts resolve difficult questions of interpretation in ways the original authors could never have imagined—this would be a tremendous accomplishment for the Iraqis, not to mention the coalition that unleashed at once the powers of democracy and anarchy, as if to see which would prevail. If a future Iraqi Supreme Court ends up declaring Iraq either an Islamic republic or a secular democratic state, it will matter little that neither outcome was intended by the equivocal, beleaguered, brave and human founders. Such a decision would, either way, signal that the constitution had done its crucial work of moving the basic question of who is in charge out of the realm of violence and into the realm of constitutional politics and its handmaiden, constitutional law. When Iraqis end up expending their energies in their own version of a contentious confirmation battle, their founding fathers and mothers will look like geniuses.

Discussion Questions for II - D

1. Diana Eck observes, with regard to the great diversity of religions in America, that diversity alone does not constitute pluralism. What is the difference between diversity and pluralism?
2. Eck also observes, "Not only is America changing these religions, but these religions are changing America." What are the implications of the cross-cultivation and hybridization for American democracy and its institutions, and for religion?
3. Martha Nussbaum advocates the use of ritual and the arts, "inspiring citizens to love . . . [democratic] values by linking the values to music, art, and ritual." And Walt Whitman, according to Nussbaum, insists that democracy needs not only laws, but also poetry to enlarge the vision of transcendence that is necessary in creating a just society. Do you agree that poetry and the other arts can and do have such an impact on the feelings and behavior of men and women? Elaborate.
4. Nussbaum, citing John Mill's religious sentiments as found in his essay, "The Religion of Humanity," believes that people can be educated to develop a moral (and civic) obligation to the common good, including tolerance for "the other." How does she propose that this moral/civic education be institutionalized?
5. Michael Walzer gives an eloquent and interesting interpretation of the book of Exodus as perennially open to interpretation and thereby immune to absolutist dogma. What, in his view, does Exodus teach us? How does his interpretation of Exodus inform our own sense of civic activism?
6. In a treatise on democracy in our time, Cornel West says, " We need a bloodstained Socratic love and tear-soaked prophetic love fueled by a hard-won tragicomic hope" to stay the course in the struggle for freedom and justice. How would you say that the wisdom of the past and the "tragicomic hope" of the blues and jazz work together as a force for democracy?
7. What prospects does El Fadl see for democracy in the Muslim world?
8. What impact has South Africa's truth and reconciliation commission, with its basic assumptions and its actions, had on the world's conflicts?
9. What strategy does Noah Feldman envision that might lead to democracy in Iraq in our time?

Contributor Notes

Abdullahi A. An-Na'im is Charles Howard Candler Professor of Law and the Director of the Religion and Human Rights Project of the Law and Religion Program at Emory University School of Law. He teaches and does research in the areas of human rights, religion, Islamic law, and criminal law. He is co-editor of *Human Rights in Africa: Cross-Cultural Perspectives* (Brookings Institution Press, 1990), and author of *Islamic Reformation: Civil Liberties, Human Rights, and International Law* (Syracuse University Press, 1990).

Mohammed Arkoun, a Berber from the mountainous region of Algeria, is an internationally renowed scholar of Islamic thought and professor emeritus at the Sorbonne. *Rethinking Islam*, published in 1994, is the first of his books to be available in English.

Peter L. Berger is University Professor of Sociology and Theology at Boston University and Director of the Institute on Culture, Religion, and World Affairs. He is author of numerous books on sociological theory, including *A Far Glory: The Quest for Faith in an Age of Credulity* (Anchor, 1993), and *Redeeming Laughter* and *Modernity, Pluralism and the Crisis of Meaning* (Walter de Gruyter, 1997).

Ian Buruma is Luce Professor of Human Rights, Democracy, and Journalism at Bard College and a fellow at the Woodrow Wilson Institute for the Humanities in Washington, D.C. He writes frequently for publications such as *The New York Times Magazine*, the *New Republic*, and the *New Yorker*. His works include *Behind the Mask* (1985), *God's Dust: A Modern Asian Journey* (1989), and *The Wages of Guilt: Memories of War in Germany and Japan* (1994).

Alan Cooperman is a *Washington Post* staff writer who covers religious issues.

Robert F. Drinan, S. J., is a professor of law at the Georgetown Law Center and was a member of Congress from Massachusetts from 1971 to 1981. Father Drinan is the author of many books and numerous articles on politics, religion, human rights and international affairs, and was the dean of the Boston College School of Law.

Diana Eck is Professor of Comparative Religion and Indian Studies at Harvard University, Master of Lowell House, and Director of The Pluralism Project. Her research focuses on religious diversity in pluralistic societies. Her book, *Encountering God: A Spiritual Journey from Bozeman to Banaras* (Beacon Press, 2003), received the Grawemeyer Book Award in 1995. In 1998, she was awarded the National Humanities Medal by President Clinton for her work on American religious diversity in The Pluralism Project.

Khaled Abou El Fadl is a Professor of Law at the UCLA School of Law. He serves on the U.S. Commission on International Religious Freedom, and is a member of the Board of Directors of Human Rights Watch. He is both an Islamic jurist and American Lawyer, and is the author of six books and numerous articles on Islamic law. His latest book is *The Place of Tolerance in Islam*.

J. Ronald Engel is Professor of Social Ethics at Meadville/Lombard Theological School and a fellow at Eco-Ethics International Union writer. He is best known for his theory on the Ecological Democratic Faith, in which he combines the interdependence of universal elements with the practical politics of democracy.

Noah Feldman is the Cecelia Goetz Professor of Law and author of *Divided By God: America's Church-State Problem—and What We Should Do About It* and numerous articles. In addition, he is Adjunct Senior Fellow at the Council on Foreign Relations.

Laurie Goodstein is a political reporter and national religion correspondent for *The New York Times*.

Irving Greenberg is president of the Jewish Life Network/Steinhart Foundation and President Emeritus and co-founder of The National Center for Learning and Leadership. A noted Jewish Studies scholar, Greenberg has served as chairman of the United States Holocaust

Memorial Museum and founder and chair of the Department of Jewish Studies at the City University of New York.

Charles Kimball is Professor of Religion and Chair of the Department of Religion at Wake Forest University. He is a lecturer and analyst on the Middle East, Islam, and the relationship between religion and politics in America. He is author of three books about religion in the Middle East.

Martin Luther King was an internationally renowned civil rights leader, orator, and author. He served as pastor at Dexter Avenue Baptist Church in Montgomery, Alabama and later co-pastor at the Ebenezer Baptist Church in Atlanta, Georgia. His notable activities include leading the Southern Christian Leadership Conference and the 1963 March on Washington. For his leadership in the United States civil rights movement, he was awarded the Nobel Peace Prize in 1964.

Dalai Lama. His Holiness the Dalai Lama is a man of peace. In 1989 he was awarded the Nobel Peace Prize for his non-violent struggle for the liberation of Tibet. He has consistently advocated policies of non-violence, even in the face of extreme aggression. He also became the first Nobel Laureate to be recognized for his concern for global environmental problems.

Mark Lilla is a Professor in the Committee on Social Thought at the University of Chicago. He is a contributor to *The New York Times* and the *New Republic*. He authored *G.B. Vico: The Making of an Anti-Modern* (Harvard University Press, 1994) and *The Reckless Mind: Intellectuals in Politics* (The New York Review of Books, 2003) and was the editor of *New French Thought: Political Philosophy* (Princeton University Press, 1994).

David Martin is Emeritus Professor of Sociology at the London School of Economics and Honorary Professor in the Department of Religious Studies at Lancaster University. He has published many books on sociology and religion, including *Tongues of Fire* (Blackwell 1990), *Does Christianity Cause War?* (1997), and *A General Theory of Secularisation* (1978).

Martha Nussbaum is the Ernst Freund Distinguished Service Professor of Law and Ethics at the University of Chicago. She was a research advisor at the World Institute for Development Economics Research in Helsinki, one of three Presidents of the American Philosophical Association, and the founder and coordinator of the Center for Comparative Constitutionalism. She has authored and edited more than twenty books including Cultivating Humanity (Harvard University Press, 1997), which won the Ness Book Award Grawemeyer Award in Education.

Michael J. Perry is the Robert W. Woodruff Professor at Emory School of Law. He held the University Distinguished Chair in Law at Wake Forest University from 1997–2003 and the Howard J. Trienens Chair in Law at Northwestern University from 1990–1997. He is one of the nation's leading scholars on the relationship of morality to law and is author of nine books, including *Love and Power: The Role of Religion and Morality in American Politics* (Cambridge University Press, 1991) and *The Idea of Human Rights: Four Inquiries* (Cambridge University Press, 1998).

Jonathan Sacks is Chief Rabbi of the United Hebrew Congregation of Britain and the Commonwealth. A regular contributor to British radio, television, and the nation press, he is the author of fourteen books and holds visiting professorships at Kings College, London, and the Hebrew University in Jerusalem.

Amartya Sen is Lamont University Professor Emeritus at Harvard University. He received the Nobel Prize in Economics in 1998 for his work on welfare economics and the Bharat Ratna in 1999. He is author of *On Economic Inequality* (Oxford University Press, 1997), and *Poverty and Famines: An Essay on Entitlement and Deprivation* (Clarendon Press, 1982).

Abdolkarim Soroush is Director of the Research Institute for the Human Sciences in Tehran, Iran. A leading Iranian and Islamic political philosopher and theologian, his principal intellect project is aimed at reconciling faith and reason, spiritual authority, and political liberty. It ranges authoritatively over comparative religion, social science and theology.

Alfred Stepan is the Wallace Sayre Professor of Government at Columbia University and a specialist in Comparative Democracy. He is the author of *Arguing Comparative Politics*, published in 2001.

Nadine Strossen is president of the American Civil Liberties Union and Professor of Law at New York Law School. She writes, lectures and practices in the areas of constitutional law, civil liberties, and international law. She is co-author of *Speaking of Race, Speaking of Sex: Hate Speech, Civil Rights, and Civil Liberties* (NYU Press, 1995) and author of *Defending Pornography: Free Speech, Sex, and the Fight for Women's Rights* (Scribner, 1995).

Desmond Tutu recipient of the Nobel Peace Prize in 1984, retired as Archbishop of Cape Town, South Africa, in 1996 and was appointed by President Nelson Mandela to chair the ground-breaking Truth and Reconciliation Commission. He is active as a lecturer throughout the world.

Michael Walzer is a permanent faculty member at the Institute for Advanced Study in Princeton, the editor of *Dissent*, and the author of *On Toleration*, published by the Yale University Press in 1997, and numerous other publications.

George Weigel is Senior Fellow at the Ethics and Public Policy Center in Washington, D.C. He is founder of the National Endowment for Democracy and was a fellow of the Woodrow Wilson International Center for Scholars in Washington, D.C. He is author or editor of seventeen books, including *Witness to Hope: The Biography of Pope John Paul II* (HarperCollins, 1999) and is a leading commentator on religious issues and public life.

Cornel West is Class of 1943 University Professor of Religion at Princeton University. The author of the contemporary classic *Race Matters*, he is the recipient of the American Book Award and has held positions at Union Theological Seminary, Yale University, Harvard University, and the University of Paris.